I0481805

THE *NEW* BUSINESS CARD

*Write and publish a book
to attract more clients, more media,
and more speaking engagements!*

Penny C. Sansevieri

Published by

ame
AUTHOR MARKETING EXPERTS

Author Marketing Experts, Inc.
P.O. Box 421156
San Diego, CA 92142
www.amarketingexpert.com

Cover by MonkeyCMedia
Interior layout by Nick Zelinger, NZ Graphics

ISBN: 978-1983546174 (softcover)
ASIN: B078RWFS95

First Edition
Printed in the USA

More books by Penny C. Sansevieri

Nonfiction
How to Sell Books by the Truckload on Amazon
(2014, 2015, 2016, 2018)
Red Hot Internet Publicity (2007, 2010, 2013, 2016)
Get Published Today (2007, 2012)
52 Ways to Sell More Books (2012, 2014)
From Book to Best-seller (2005, 2007)
No More Rejections: Get Published Today!
(Infinity Publishing, 2002, 2003)
Get Published! An Author's Guide to the Online Publishing Revolution
(1st Books, 2001)

Fiction
Candlewood Lake (iUniverse, 2005)
The Cliffhanger (iUniverse, 2000)

To subscribe to our free newsletter, send an email to
subscribe@amarketingexpert.com

We'd love your feedback.
Here's how to contact us:

Author Marketing Experts, Inc.
P.O. Box 421156
San Diego, CA 92142
www.amarketingexpert.com

CONTENTS

SECTION THREE:
GETTING READY TO GO TO MARKET

Section One

Why a Book Will Change Your (Business) Life

In the coming pages, you will learn ways to unearth all of your options and opportunities. You will learn tactics and techniques on how to pull in new dollars in the form of leads from the book, sales of the book, and sales of products you may create as a result of writing this book. The only thing you need to decide is this: How big do you want your business to be?

Bottom line, no matter how big or small your business is, you should always be on the lookout for ways to increase your revenue. You might decide to launch new products or services, or raise your prices, or you could do a combination of both. But the there is often a cap for the number of times you can introduce new products or raise prices. You can only create so many products before you confuse your end user, and you can only raise your prices so often before you price yourself right out of the market.

The techniques I am going to share with you in this book are vastly different from either of the methods mentioned above, because they come from a different perspective. Your first step will be to look at your business differently—and I want you to look at it from the 30,000-foot-high perspective, the wide view. In other words, it's time to look at all the facets, and all elements of of your business.

We are going to look at each and every one of the million little pieces that make up your business and fold this knowledge into your successful, sought-after book.

Many of the ideas I will share with you have come from my own personal experience. When I first started Author Marketing Experts, Inc., I had no marketing budget, no advertising budget, and virtually no revenue to speak of. In fact, I started my business after a rather unexpected turn of events in my life—I was laid off from a company that I was expecting to be with for at least another ten years.

That was eighteen years ago. I started my company with the idea that I would be a consulting firm and nothing but. As I dug deeper into the industry, I realized there was more I could offer, and more paths to increasing my company's revenue streams beyond consulting fees.

So I wrote a book. From there, I was able to design products, one to hand out like business cards, and ones to sell, and it was these new products which started driving people to my company.

You'll begin creating your *New Business Card* by taking an in-depth look at your business and your goals, while making decisions about where you'd like your company to go. Your goal could be that of a local business interested in creating areas of revenue that serve a national market. Or it may not. You may not be interested in a national market, or maybe you've never even considered it a possibility. But now you can.

While you're doing this first step, use the first rule of successful brainstorming: leave no stone unturned. No idea is too wild or "out there" to be considered.

Maximizing Your Revenue

When I speak to business groups about maximizing revenue, they are often confused by the direction my workshop takes them. When you talk about maximizing revenue, most business owners automatically think *I need to raise my prices!* But we're going to go in a completely different direction.

Maximizing revenue is about finding and creating tools to help you maximize your existing customer base/platform. This is not marketing per se, but a different way to grab attention.

For the purposes of this book, we are going to look at things that I call "drivers." These are items or activities that help to drive consumer attention back to your product or service that you're selling.

Consumers are overwhelmed. They have a million choices and just as many purchase options. The key is to find ways to rise above the noise. A lot of marketing people will talk to you about social media and other forms of online marketing. I think online marketing is great, and social media is definitely something that everyone in business should utilize. But if you're driving people to your website by using social media, how are you enticing them to stay there and take the time to get acquainted with you, your company, your products?

Maybe they want to get to know you first, which is totally understandable. A book is a great way to introduce yourself, your business philosophy, your organization, and your products to those future customers.

In another book I wrote, *Red Hot Internet Publicity*, we talk about website development and design, so for now let's assume your site is doing a good job of converting your customers. Let's assume you already do some form of marketing, both online and off. Right now it doesn't matter what that is. The tools you learn here will also help you market your business in a different way.

These days, consumers are looking for content—helpful, insightful, informative content. In order to remain relevant, you need to not only stay on top of your market, but also offer content to your consumer. Content can take many forms: it can be paid or unpaid; it can be video, infographics, or printed matter.

Maximizing revenue is about putting more pieces in place to help you drive more attention to your business, and increase the visibility of your products, services, or books.

Educate Instead of Sell

One of the best ways to market yourself or your business is to educate instead of sell. People are very sensitive to being hustled, and often don't like to be hit with pushy sales tactics. Studies have shown that only 3 percent of people actually want to buy when they meet you or land on your site. This small number says you can bet that most people landing on your website aren't going to buy the first time around.

When you educate or inform your site visitors, you build loyalty. They come to you for information and guidance; you become their resource. When they are ready to buy, guess who they will think of first?

Most people in business are very tactical. They want to make the sale—that's it. Yes, of course we all want to make the sale, but if you've picked up this book, you are likely more than just a tactical person, you are also a strategist.

What does it mean to be a strategist? It means you have long-term business goals. You aren't just interested in making a sale today; you want to become the company your customer goes to whenever they have the need for what you offer. Whether your business provides consulting or sells printers, you can still weave this education strategy into everything you do. Building these systems into your business (i.e. writing a book and creating additional products as necessary) is also a great way to keep momentum going all the time, not just when ads or promotions are running. In this type of a scenario, a book keeps working and keeps marketing for you. It's truly your 24/7 sales tool.

A New Way to Look at Your Business to Develop Your Leads Funnel

In order for you to begin this process, and transform yourself from salesperson to strategist, I want you to start looking at your business from a new angle.

First, look at your existing product. If you're selling a service, take a closer look at the service and identify the different points of entry. Where does your customer encounter your message? Is it on your website? Via your social media?

Also, I want you to look at your immediate needs. If you've picked up this book, your immediate needs likely include attracting more customers, doing more public speaking, adding more media exposure, and drumming up new business. Unfortunately, those goals are much too broad. I want you to narrow your focus and take a more microscopic look at *your customer.*

'What does my consumer really need? What drives them to me and, perhaps most important, what's their pain point?' Pain point, simply put, is the reason they come to you—whether that means that they want to be entertained or want something delivered. They have a need and that's your pain point.

'What problem do I solve for my customers?' Defining what your end user needs will help you define or redefine how you market to them. To help break this down even further, I'd like you to answer some questions before we move on. Your answers will give you a little more clarity about where your consumers' hot buttons are, which will in turn, help you create your book. Your answers can be as brief or as lengthy as you want, and if you need more room for your answers, grab a blank sheet of paper.

*Who is my ideal consumer? (give a brief example phrase, as you
do in the third question; i.e. a fanatical housekeeper on the alert
for bargains...joke, but you get my drift)*

_____

_____

_____

_____

_____

What are their needs as they relate to my service or product?
(brief example phrase; i.e. clear instructions for how to use it
for maximum benefit)

_____

_____

_____

_____

_____

What are some of their emotional hot buttons?
(In other words, what will drive them to buy this?)

_____

_____

_____

_____

What is their biggest immediate need?

_____

_____

_____

_____

_____

After going through this exercise, we sometimes unearth new buying motives or consumer hot buttons they had not previously considered. Let me give you an example, using a company you would never expect would have to search for ways to maximize revenue.

I once walked into a hardware store in New York, where I lived at the time. It was a great store in the Village. The problem was that a brand-spanking-shiny-new Home Depot was opening near Central Park (granted, it was a hike from the hardware store in the Village). Over time, the Village store noticed their customer base falling off. After looking at what the other guys were doing differently, they noticed that the other guys were not only selling a bigger selection of items but personalized service as well.

So what could this small store do to attract more people to their business? When they analyzed the needs of their customer, they realized that a high percentage of their customers were women, many of them younger, trying to save a bit of money here and there, and hoping to fix a leak or some other small problem in their apartment. Plumbers and handymen in New York can be pretty pricey, so I suggested that the store host do-it-yourself classes for local residents, and also create a series of easy and short how-to books their shoppers could quickly thumb through to help them do the job themselves. They loved the idea.

But then I added another idea to the mix: I told them to record the classes and put them up on YouTube. Especially with something like a home fix-it, it's often easier for people to view the how-to video on their computer screens than read it in a book. Viewers can stop and start the video while they work through the process. To top it off, the book would be a natural accompaniment to the video.

Once they created books and videos, I encouraged them to take it one step further by putting together a newsletter. They were already collecting signups so converting this into a mailing list was easy for them to do. The newsletter offered money-saving tips such as energy conservation or DIY ideas, promoted new books they were publishing, and included a schedule of their upcoming live classes, along with a link to their YouTube channel.

Within a month, their business spiked again. Why did this happen? Because they tapped directly into their customers' needs. They weren't just a hardware store anymore. They had become a resource.

Sure, there will always be people who gravitate to the big, shiny stores, but in a neighborhood like the Village, most folks would rather buy local. Also, if you know New York at all, you know that unless you have a car (which most people don't), hauling anything on the subway can be a chore.

This store became a key resource on top of fulfilling their original need of being a store. Their website traffic kicked up, which helped bring in even more new customers. The classes all used in-store staff as instructors, and often customers would come in with questions directed at the staffer who taught the video class. The videos personalized their buying experience in a way where staffers were often asked for by name. This creates a personal, connected experience with your customer, and can greatly increase buyer loyalty.

In another example, I worked with a business owner who desperately wanted to begin public speaking. We pitched him to a number of speaking gigs, and every one of them asked, "Does he have a book?" He didn't. And he also didn't get the gigs. A year later he went back, book in hand, and got more speaker bookings than he could handle.

Sometimes additional revenue can result from a very simple tweak in your marketing. Sometimes it will require you to step outside your comfort zone in a way you had not previously considered. Other times a slight change in what you are already doing can work magic.

Now, let's look at how you can start maximizing your revenue… right away!

I Don't Have Time to Write a Book

A lot of books out there talk about how to maximize time, how to accomplish more during your day, and so on. The truth is, time still seems to fly, no matter how carefully you manage it. If you're already starting to think, "I don't have time to write a book," then think again.

You don't have time *not* to write a book.

As business owners, most of us already have content, whether we realize it or not. Perhaps you've written white papers, blog posts, or other articles. You may even have some guides you created for staff training that can be massaged into a book.

Of course you can always use a ghostwriter if you truly are too busy. Ghostwriting, or ghosting, is a fantastic way to get a book done quickly, and I'll cover more of that in the chapter *Hiring Someone Else to Write Your Book*. And if you're worried about the ghost knowing your "voice," keep in mind it's what they do. I've had a book ghost-written, and I bet you can't guess which one (here's a hint; it's not the one you're reading). Ghosting is a fantastic resource for any business owner, and if it means the difference between getting a book out there and not, it's a great investment.

If you don't believe me, consider this: in the nearly eighteen years I've been running Author Marketing Experts, Inc., I have never run a single ad. Ninety-percent of our business has come from my books, or associated content that I developed as a result of a book I wrote. Did it pay off? Yes, it did. In the early years, it helped us double our revenue every year. After a while it levels out, of course, but it shouldn't stop. We currently increase our revenue 20-30% every year without the use of any advertisements. The tools work if you make time to create them.

How Do People Find
Your Business?

Most business owners don't have a clue how their customers find them. That's okay if you don't know. After all, you have been too busy running your business, right?

Well, now it's time to work *on* your business instead of *in* it. Before you can dig into creating and offering consumer content, you first have to ask yourself, in detail, how *do* people find you?

Social Media

Like most business owners, you might have been dragged into social media kicking and screaming. I have friends who have run businesses for years who have never touched LinkedIn, Twitter, or Facebook. It's just not what they are into. Let's assume your business is on social media. While coaching business owners, I found that 90% of them didn't have a clue about whether or not social media was actually paying off for them. It was something they did because everyone else does. If you find yourself in this category, that's fine.

Referrals

Clients of yours telling friends about you is a great way to get new business and, candidly, the easiest. Make the most of these amazing referrals!

Website Leads

If you are getting leads from your website, great! We'll look at how you can increase your site's effectiveness. If you're not getting leads from your website, I will walk you through how to make it happen.

Newsletter

If you have a newsletter, it's probably emailed to your audience and (hopefully) generating leads for you. If you don't have one, I will make a case for why you should.

Speaking Events/Networking

If you're a speaker, you probably get a lot of leads from events where you present. If you aren't a speaker, but attend industry events, you probably get a certain number of leads just from networking. Which is great, but unless you're going to networking events every week (and who has time for that?), it probably isn't an ongoing or lucrative source of lead generation for you.

What are some the other ways people can find you?

List some of them here. It will be important to keep them handy so you can figure out how they can be maximized:

_____

_____

_____

_____

_____

_____

_____

_____

Becoming a Creator

Owning a successful business these days can be complicated and challenging. Not only do you have to run the business and manage the staff (unless you're a solo-preneur), but the demands on your time will also seem endless and overwhelming. We don't often see ourselves as "creators." We are business owners and entrepreneurs—but creators?

After all, who has time to create?

You do.

Become a creator of content—helpful, insightful, unique content that will capture your consumers' attention , which, as you well know, isn't easy.

Remember, consumers don't want to be hustled. In fact, they hate it. Think about yourself: you are a consumer, too. Don't you hate being pressured by sales associate? I went to a seminar with a fantastic speaker once ... that is, until he spent the last twenty minutes of his presentation selling me on his product and telling me why, if I didn't buy his product right now, I would probably fail at everything I do. Well, he didn't put it quite like that, but you get the idea. Hard-selling defeats the whole purpose of educating and creating a returning loyal customer. You might as well save yourself time and just get straight to your sales pitch.

Becoming a Resource

In the current business environment, it's important to become a resource. Consumers no longer want to be sold, they want to be informed. When people think of your industry, they think of you, yes? If you're not sure, creating content (i.e. a book) will help position you as the go-to person for all things related to your industry.

How to Create Great Content

The best ideas for content won't come from you, but rather from the needs of your market. How do you unearth these ideas? Ask yourself some in-depth questions about your potential customers. We've already covered some of this so before you think that your answers may seem redundant, it's important to answer all of them and, if possible, push yourself to answer them in different ways.

For example, most businesses don't have just one reason why people contact them. Even if you run a speedy messenger service, there isn't just one reason someone will want to hire you. Aside from the known needs of wanting something delivered and it also to be done quickly, but there could be other reasons. It could be save time, to close that mega-important deal or to help them grow their business? If they're running around doing their own deliveries, they aren't going to have time to build their business.

I want you to inspect your consumer from every angle, like you would with a prism, so you can get a thorough, complete sense of what their real needs are. I encourage you to do this exercise multiple times. Every time, you'll be able to dig deeper into your market's needs, and that's exactly where you want to be.

Why do they need my product or service?

_____

_____

_____

_____

_____

What motivates them to buy from me or another provider?

_____

_____

_____

_____

_____

What problem does my product or service solve?

_____

_____

_____

_____

_____

Why is my service or product better than my competition?

_____

_____

_____

_____

_____

What's the biggest change I foresee in this market?

_____

_____

_____

_____

_____

How will this affect my business?

_____

_____

_____

_____

_____

Is there a trend that affects what and/or how much I sell?
If so, what is it?

_____

_____

_____

_____

_____

How does this trend matter to my business?

_____

_____

_____

_____

_____

Now you have a better sense of what your customer needs, let's dig into creating some action steps for your book.

Spycraft

If you want to write a really good book (and why wouldn't you?), then you should consider doing some spy work. Make a list of all the top books in your industry (let's say you pick the top 10 or so), and take a look at the reviews on Amazon. Read about what people love, though lots of five-star reviews may just be people gushing (we love gushing, but it does not tell us a lot about the book). Find the reviews that weren't that great, or maybe offered the author some solid feedback. For example, "I wish there had been more of X" or "I would like to see the author address XYZ." Lots of similar feedback will often point you in the direction of material that may need to be covered in your book, or give you some tips for creating something that speaks more directly to the current needs of your potential customer!

Putting it All Together

Now we've looked at your business, your leads, and your customers. Let's take a closer look at creating the structure and identifying content you could incorporate into your book or books.

What Do You Want to Accomplish?

Now I've thrown out a ton of options, it's time for you to decide what you want to accomplish by publishing a book. Is it to get more business? Book more speaking engagements? Gain more media exposure? It may be all of these things, but it's important to define what your goals are as they relate to this project. Then you'll be able to craft something that supports and nourishes your specific needs.

Let's say you're a dog trainer and you want to do more public speaking. You'll want to include a section in the back of your book that tells people what topics you can speak on and how to reach you. So, for example, you could break your topics down like this:

Dog Training

- 20-minute address covers common challenges in owning a dog, basics of establishing a workable relationship, and a couple of easy training exercises.

- 35-40 minute address, including everything in the 20-minute discussion, plus integrating a new puppy if you already have another dog, quick and easy house-training tips, and easy commands the entire family can learn and benefit from!

- (Slide show and video are optional)

This breaks it down, in some detail. Always keep in mind that if this is how someone is choosing whether to invite you to speak for them, then being more specific in terms of your speaker offerings is likely get you more speaking engagements!

If your goal is to get more customers, include a coupon for something free. Maybe it's a free consultation, or a free thirty-minute tech session. It's important to be in tune with what the rest of your market is doing. Remember that to pull a book together is a fantastic accomplishment. Don't let that get in the way of creating a book that will work for you, too. Let it bring in more clients or customers.

Content, Content, Content

Now it's time to see what you've already got on hand for your book. I suggest going through your existing content to see what can be repurposed. Consider these items as possible ways to gather content:

- blog posts
- white papers
- audio and/or video recordings
- presentations you've done in the past
- class and presentation handouts
- articles written for publications or other blogs
- newsletters
- Twitter updates (because these might help spawn book content, too)

Gather all of this content together and see what fits with the book and what does not. You may be surprised by how much content you already have on hand.

Need to Find a Good Assistant?

If becoming a published author is adding a layer of work you just don't have the time for, consider hiring a VA (virtual assistant). If you're ready to go the Virtual Assistant route, consider going to the International Virtual Assistants Organization www.ivaa.org/ and post your job there.

If you'd rather hire an intern, you can find interns by placing detailed job descriptions here: Internweb.com & Internjobs.com

Section Two

Let's Get Published!

"The way to get started is to quit talking and begin."
– Walt Disney

Defining Your Goals

*"For several days after my first book was published,
I carriedit about in my pocket and took surreptitious
peeps at it to make sure the ink had not faded."*
– Sir J.M. Barrie

When starting a business, you'd never open your doors without having inventory in stock, or services and pricing ready to go, right? Yet it's amazing to me how often I see authors launch a book without goals or a plan. Remember that hope is not a marketing plan. You have to have a plan, even if it's still evolving. A book as a business card is good, but a book with a marketing plan is better. Knowing your goals for publishing will go a long way to directing you to your correct destination.

For some of us, publishing is about getting your stuff "out there." You want to see it in print so you can find out if it has legs that can help you expand your business. Or you want to publish to garner more spfseceaking gigs. For others it's a bigger project, a life's dream, and a chance at expanding their media reach and national exposure.

For most of us, however, our books are our business card, meaning that it's a way to attract more people to your store, business, or consulting services. Whatever your goal, it's best to define it early on. Why? Because it will affect every decision you make, from how to publish to how to promote.

In order to determine how you will publish, and then how much you'll spend on marketing, you need to know where you're going. For example, if your goal is to use the book to help build your business, then marketing to media might not be your goal. You might be better off gathering steam online, and finding your audience and customers that way. If you've written a book just to reach a deeper online market, and drive more people to your website and store, then it doesn't matter how or what time of year you publish. In fact, you could even e-publish the book. So figure out what it is you really want and then outline a plan accordingly.

Take a few moments to answer the following questions. They will help you determine your goals, and help you dig deeper into your market and focus.

Answering these questions will be a real eye-opener for most. Honest answers will reveal areas you need to focus on. This focus can help you get as much out of this book as you can. Then, when you've finished reading this book, go back and answer them again and see how you do. I'm certain you'll be amazed at your progress.

- Why do I want to write a book?
- What elements of my business do I want to enhance/grow with this book?
- Am I interested in doing speaking engagements?
- Do I have a passion for my work, and will others feel my passion?
- Can I wear the many hats of an entrepreneur and publisher?
- Can I engage others to help me produce and sell my books?
- Is my book a stand-alone, part of a series of books, or maybe a way to launch more products?
- How can I make my book different from others already published on my subject?
- Can I set clear goals and follow a plan?

One of the best assets you can have is to know your limitations. Face it: we all have them. Knowing what they are and dealing with them in advance will put us a step ahead of the process. Not acknowledging them and not addressing them will take precious time, attention and energy away from your project, and sometimes operate "behind your back," to sabotage your efforts.

Publishing Overview:
The Business of Publishing

*"Publishing a volume of verse is like dropping a rose petal
down the Grand Canyon and waiting for the echo."*
– Don Marquis

The truth is this: publishing is a business like any other. In this case, your book is the product. And you need to learn how to set up that product to bring in revenue. We'll get into this more, and look at what sells and why in just a minute. For now, let's dig deeper into traditional publishing.

Traditional publishing, also called corporate publishing, legacy publishing, or New York publishing, was for many years the only way to go. For business authors, I strongly encourage you to consider going the self-publishing route, but let's outline the options first so you understand your choices.

The Publishers

Publishing falls into two broad categories: traditional and independent (also referred to as self- or indie publishing). The term "independent" can also encompass boutique publishers, as well as print on demand.

New York and Books

When we think of publishing, we tend to default to the big publishers in New York. There's a good reason for this: 90% of the books you see in bookstores are actually created on an island: the island of Manhattan. Also referred to as corporate, trade, or traditional publishing, the big five in New York have virtually owned the market on best sellers, though a few best sellers have recently proven that even an independent title can hit the best-seller lists.

When we speak of "traditional" publishing, we're talking about publishers who pay for the right to publish your work. This means they pay you an advance by purchasing all the "rights" to your work. This can include foreign rights, movie rights, paperback rights, and so on. It also means you sign over any creative license. In essence, once you sign with a publisher, they (the publisher) can decide that your book should be sold to a different market, or that chapters need to be pulled or reorganized. You no longer have a say. Does that sound scary to you? Well, depending on who you ask, it can be.

So why do most of us prefer this route to publishing? Because publishers absorb all the costs, right?

Well, not really. These days, while publishers do pay for production, the cost of marketing is squarely on the authors' shoulders. That's right. Aside from national distribution, most publishers don't provide a lot of support, especially in the areas of marketing and publicity. Distribution is another important factor to consider.

Facts about Trade/Traditional Publishing

Here are some facts that might surprise you:

First, a book that sells 10,000 copies is considered a major success. Was this always the case? No. But with the number of books crowding the market, that's a significant number, unless you are Stephen King, Nora Roberts, Dean Koontz or James Patterson.

Trade publishing is driven by hit titles. On average, 10 percent of new books generate 90 percent of a publisher's profits. What does this mean for you? Well, publishers like to go after "star" authors, big names who can carry the list. For example, several of Seth Godin's books were considered star titles, but mostly for the business division of Penguin, which is the house he was signed with at the time. Few, if any, business books carry an entire publishing house the way fiction might. Tim Ferris's *The 4-Hour Workweek* was considered a star title, and could carry an entire publishing house. If publishers have 90 percent so-so selling books but 10 percent major titles, they are considered a success. This means, that if you are in the 90 percent of what they consider so-so titles, you probably won't get the lion's share of attention from their marketing department, if any at all. What do I mean by "so-so" title? It's a title that may or may not sell well, despite the work that's been done on the book and its estimated market.

If a book needs work, traditional publishing editors these days don't have the time to devote to major revisions. What does this mean to you? It means if you're submitting a book to anyone from publisher to agent, it must be clean. Get it edited, vetted, whatever you need to do to eliminate the work the agent/publisher/editor needs to do to get it to market. You might think your title is original, but for every book idea submitted, a hundred other similar titles are waiting to be approved, so despite the originality of your idea, the competition can still be fierce.

Publishers expect authors to participate in (if not run) their own marketing campaigns. Regardless of how you publish, these days you will be your own marketing department. Do not expect a publishing house to take the reins of your campaign.

Books by the Numbers

The average book sells 250 copies.

4,500 new books are published daily.

Big publishers prefer big names (remember that 10% rule).

38 percent of books are now sold online.

Amazon has 71 percent of the eBook market.

Sources: Publisher's Weekly, BISAC, The Hot Sheet

Different Ways to Publish a Book

"Writing is one of the few professions in which you can psychoanalyze yourself, get rid of hostilities and frustrations in public, and get paid for it."
– Octavia Butler

We've already discussed the traditional way to publish a book. But it's not the only way. Self-publishing covers a variety of ways to publish, so before we move on, it's important to define which type of publishing is right for you and your book.

Vanity Publishing Explained

The term "vanity publishing" came out of a series of companies who were set up, dozens of years ago, to publish your book for a very high fee. You'd pay them, let's say $7,000, and they'd create a book cover, book interior, and maybe (if you're lucky) pop it up on Amazon for you. And while most of these companies have long since gone away, a few still remain, which is why it's good to vet your publishing options before you sign on the dotted line. Because $7,000 can get you a lot of book publishing and marketing if you spend the money in the right way.

Self-Publishing – Print on Demand

Print-on-Demand (POD) is a way to publish your book easily and economically. What this means is you choose and hire a publisher, you pay a fee, and they publish your book. You still keep all rights to the book, but the process of creating a book, putting it up on Amazon, and getting it into various sales systems are all part of what the publisher will do for you.

Self-Publishing – Print Books - Becoming Your Own Publisher

When you decide to become your own publisher, all the responsibility of layout, book cover design, distribution, and even the relationship with Amazon, iTunes, Barnes & Noble, Baker and Taylor (a book wholesaler), and more, rests on your shoulders. It might seem like a lot of work, but many authors enjoy publishing this way, since they have more control over the process. They also understand that a print on demand publisher has very limited distribution. Meaning that you won't get national placement in bookstores or Costco (though, frankly, most books from traditional publishers don't get this either). If you are new to your particular market, and perhaps you are unsure of the sales potential of your book, then it might be a good idea to test the market with print on demand, and then self-publish the book after you have built a solid publishing model.

Self-Publishing – E-books

For many of us, e-books are just another way to make our book available to an even larger, electronic-focused market. E-book technology has made great strides over the years, and e-books continue to rise in popularity. If you choose to publish only the e-book, you can certainly do that. But my recommendation is to have a book available in all different formats, and through different outlets, including Amazon, iTunes, Barnes & Noble, and Draft2Digital; that way you have a book that's accessible on the Kindle, iPad or any other e-book reader that might come along.

Traditional Publishing

If you get picked up by a publisher, you sign a contract which means that, you will essentially sign over all the rights to your book. The publisher is responsible for everything from the cover, to editing, to the interiors and sometimes (if you're extremely lucky) the marketing. Sometimes, traditional publishers may even pick up a self-published book if it's achieved enough momentum.

What New York Publishers Do Best

In this day and age, you can bypass the traditional publisher, but you shouldn't bypass their strategy, and here's why. The New York set does a lot of things well, the first of which is the cover. They hire the best cover designers, the best interior designers, and their books are often edited several times. You can shortcut the system by self-publishing, but you should never shortcut their methods. For your book to have a fighting chance, it needs to look, and be, polished and professional. Don't publish a science project. Seriously.

Going Digital with E-books

"Books are no more threatened by Kindle than stairs by elevators."
– Stephen Fry

We've already discussed the traditional way to publish a book. hat is relatively inexpensive to produce, has a quick turnaround production time, and is evergreen? In the publishing world, we're talking about e-books. Once was mostly unknown and obscure documents with limited distribution, e-books in many cases now outsell hardcover and paperback books.

Though this is a fact that mainstream publishers would have you believe otherwise. A recent piece on the Money Track at CNN.com cited that e-reader sales declined 40% between 2011 and 2016 and many mainstream publishers will suggest that e-book sales are dropping. With that statement, herald the welcome back of print books! Print books are alive and well!

And indeed they are, but the problem here is, though e-readers may be declining, we see a surge in e-reader apps being downloaded. People want fewer devices, so they're reading on their iPads or phones. This piece, in *Fortune Magazine,* clearly describes the issue at hand:

> Some of the e-book slump amounts to chickens coming home to roost for traditional publishers. They have been fighting to keep e-book prices high—to the point where they engaged in industry-wide collusion with Apple in an attempt to do so— and they eventually managed to convince Amazon to let them set prices. Is it really such a surprise that higher prices lead to people buying fewer e-books?

But that's only half the story. According to the figures from Author Earnings—which are based in part on regular samples of Amazon sales data—what's really been happening is that the market share of established publishers has been declining, while sales of independently published e-books have been growing. In particular, sales of books that don't even have industry standard ISBN numbers have increased.

The phenomenon of e-books is due to several factors: the creation of inexpensive, portable, easy-to-use e-reader devices and smart phone applications; an incredibly fast production time; and a rise in the number of independent publishers and self-publishers who capitalized on this perfect storm.

Digital books have been around a lot longer than many people realize, but it wasn't until the convergence of the Internet and technology in 2009 that e-books and e-readers hit the mainstream, and accustomed book buyers to the delights of instant gratification.

Major players include Amazon's Kindle, the Sony Reader, Barnes & Noble's Nook, and Apple's iPad tablet. Now most smart phones also offer free apps for many of these e-readers, which makes them ever more accessible to an even larger audience of consumers who can— and do—buy and read e-books any time. Now many authors are using e-books as a creative and enhanced way to drive more attention to their print books, or even as stand-alone titles. Let's explore some creative ways authors are using e-books.

Why Have an E-book?

First off, let's look at potential "whys" that a consumer may ask of an e-book. Why would you want one? Well, there's an excellent chance that a large portion of your audience loves to read electronically. I you're going to sell books and reach a bigger market, it's probably a good idea to get the book out in as many different formats as you can.

Another thing to consider is that e-books are normally less expensive to produce, and therefore more cost-effective than print books, in terms of printing and delivery. This will allow you to do a lot more for your investment, and offer more to readers in terms of pricing.

The Discoverability of E-books

Often I'll see authors use their e-book to drive attention to their print book. They may be doing this because they already know they have a larger audience for printed books than e-book readers. Using a shorter e-book version for e-book discount days and e-book promotions (freebie or discounts) is a great way to drive interest to your existing title and to your overall brand. And like anything we see float across our screens, if it's something we want, we'll click on the link to find out more. Even if you believe your market is largely print-directed, print readers browsing the Internet will still click through to see what other formats you have available if it's something they want.

Book Bundles

Book bundling came into "fashion" about two years ago, mostly due to the romance market (an excellent genre to watch, since romances continue to outsell every other niche or genre combined). If you look at the romance category on Amazon, you can't help but notice e-book bundles. These are books that are bundled together and sold under a single title. They can include two books or, in some cases, twenty or more. I mention this, because if you have more books that you've done, or might be doing in the future, you could also bundle them to release as a "set" on Amazon.

All you need is the interior book file, or e-book file if you have access to it. If you've already published the e-books you plan to bundle, you should be familiar enough with Amazon, Barnes & Noble, and other platforms to combine and upload the content of each book.

You'll need a new cover for the bundle and to find out how to include the cover of each included book right before the content.

Overcoming Objections

When I published *Red Hot Internet Publicity*, I also wanted to do an e-book. The only problem was it contains a workbook, and it's a bit difficult to fill out the workbook pages on an e-reader or a Kindle App. I solved this by offering a link to a hidden page on my website where readers can download the workbook and, in the process, I collect their email addresses for my newsletter. Be sure to mention to your readers first that you'll be adding them to your newsletter distribution list!

There may be several reasons why you don't think your book will work in digital. Maybe it's a coffee table book. Okay, coffee table books may not be a great idea for an e-reader, but how about a companion guide to the coffee table version, such as a discussion guide about the photography in the coffee table book? This works well, especially when it's a travel-related book, because you have more space to elaborate on the photography than you would in a big coffee table book.

A companion guide, at its most basic, is an enhancement for your print book. Companion guides can take the form of workbooks, reader guides, pretty much anything you want as a "companion" to your book and will allow the reader to enhance their experience. Companion guides are a great way to take a really pricey book, like a coffee table book, and make it more accessible. If done right, a less pricey companion guides can drive folks to the higher-priced book. There are markets where books are priced higher just because it's what the market will bear, such as real estate and finance. It's not an easy thing to drive readers to a $35- or $65-dollar book, but far easier to whet their appetite by offering a less pricey version to lead them to your bigger, more profitable book!

When you have so many possibilities for publishing, looking at all your options is crucial if you want to maximize effectiveness and profit. You now have the opportunity to sell your book in a variety of different formats, and you should consider all of them, because you never know where the next sale might come from.

How Quickly Can You Publish?

Amazon offers a service called Kindle Direct Publishing, or KDP. Once you have your file converted (to publish on Amazon, you need a .MOBI or Word format), you then upload the book file, the cover—and your book could be live on Amazon within 24 hours! Depending on your book pricing, you could also get up to a 70% royalty on each sale.

If you'd like to learn more about KDP, visit their site: kdp.amazon.com.

Where to Sell Your E-book

It's easy to feel overwhelmed by all the options available for selling your book. You could simplify it, however, by publishing straight to Amazon to start. And I encourage you to do it that way. Why? I mean, wouldn't you want to have your book on Barnes & Noble, Kobo, iTunes and other outlets?

Well, yes and no. For your market, you'll see the lion's share of e-book sales on Amazon, as opposed to Nook or Kobo. According to AuthorEarnings.com, Amazon accounts for 74% of all US e-book purchases. And while both of the other platforms offer great opportunities, going exclusively with Amazon, at least initially, has its benefits. Let me explain.

When you sign up with Kindle Direct Publishing, you have the option of signing exclusively with them for 90 days. During those 90 days, you can't have the book listed anywhere else for that period of time. During that time, however, you have the opportunity to do some e-book giveaways, which can help boost sales of the book.

But how can free e-books help boost paid sales? Two reasons: first of all, a free e-book creates a certain amount of momentum, and when the book goes back to paid status, that momentum carries through and helps to boost the book's exposure. The second reason is that there are a lot of book- and reader-oriented sites out there who will give you some great exposure, but they will only list your book during a free promotion. Keep in mind that I'm not encouraging you to offer your book for free for a long period of time. If the promo is done correctly, one or two days are all you need to help spike your sales.

My book, *How to Sell Books by the Truckload,* on Amazon explains several ways to optimize your e-book promotion.

Here are some of the places that will help you publish your e-book:

Amazon: Given all of the Kindle-related groups online for authors, Kindle fanatics, and Kindle book deals, Amazon is a great place to start, and offers a 70% royalty program if your book is priced $2.99 or higher. kdp.amazon.com/self-publishing/help.

Draft2Digital: With a setup similar to Smashwords, Draft2Digital is a great resource for publishing your book on a variety of platforms, including Amazon, iTunes/Apple's iBookstore, Kobo, Barnes & Noble, Sony, Diesel, Aldiko—all with one click of a button. It's also quite possibly the easiest platform to use. www.draft2digital.com/steps/

BookBaby: This site will allow you to sell your book through Apple, Kindle, Nook and Sony. There is a sign-up fee that covers the conversion to e-book format. www.bookbaby.com/book-distribution

Nook: Use Nook Press to self publish and reach their audience. www.nookpress.com/

Apple: Self-publish through iTunes Connect Online.
itunesconnect.apple.com/WebObjects/iTunesConnect.
woa/wa/apply
www.apple.com/itunes/working-itunes/sell-content/
books/book-faq.html

Since e-books never go out of print, you can always find an audience once you've got your e-book online. Consider some of the following resources for information on all things Kindle.

- Amazon Kindle Book Forum – for authors and Kindle lovers
  www.amazon.com/forum/kindle
- Nook boards – for e-book readers and authors
  www.nookboards.com/forum/
- Kindleboards (kboards) – Kindle fans can learn about what's going on, and authors can share information and tips
  www.kindleboards.com/
- Yahoo Kindle Group – less author opportunity, more of a Kindle fan forum
  groups.yahoo.com/group/kindlekorner/

There are many websites devoted to free or low-priced e-books, providing plenty of opportunities for authors to promote their books, including:

- Ignite your Book – free and deeply discounted e-books
  www.igniteyourbook.com/
- BookGorilla – free and deeply discounted e-books (they're also part of Kindle Nation Daily, and often buying an add-on Kindle Nation Daily will also boost you on BookGorilla).
  www.bookgorilla.com
- Kindle Nation Daily – free books, tips and news
  kindlenationdaily.com/

- Pixel of Ink – free and bargain Kindle books
  www.pixelofink.com/
- Ereader News Today – tips, tricks and free Kindle e-books
  ereadernewstoday.com/
- eReader IQ – free Kindle books
  www.ereaderiq.com/free/

Hardcover or Softcover?

Most authors with the dream of having a hardcover version of their book, but is it really worth it? Typically, hardcover is surprisingly more expensive than paperback, and far more expensive than an e-book. Dollar for dollar, it is unlikely to net out in your favor. You may argue that you're in a market that is heavily hardcover, but even if you sell well, your profit margin is directly relational to whether you choose to go with hardcover or not. Consider your options, and then make a decision based on what will best serve the needs of both you and your book.

Going Audio

We hear so much about e-books these days, that it is easy to forget that long before the e-book, there was another alternative to reading books: audio. If you talk with audiobook lovers, you'll find they are passionate about their books, and most can't recall the last time they actually sat down to read a print or e-book as opposed to listening to one. I spoke to some cross-country truck drivers who go through as many as five books a month. What do they listen to? Anything from world history to self-help to fiction.

Audible has been around for a long time, and we see still deals offering three months free everywhere. Even better, Audible's technology, Whispersync, has made some great advancements. It allows people to both read and listen to books with either the book or the audio version discounted when you buy the other option. This kind of format is quickly becoming unstoppable and will be interesting to watch how this product will mold the next generation of book delivery.

Additionally, about three years ago Amazon launched ACX, which is a means for anyone to turn their book into an audio product. Perhaps the most surprising aspect is, it takes very little effort. I'll walk you through the actual process of turning your book into an audio product. First, let's look at a few tips I gleaned from research, authors, and from a couple of the readers whose voices you hear in audiobooks:

Hire a Narrator

If you've ever listened to an audiobook, you already know the narrator can make or break a story. I was listening to a book recently and, though I liked the information, I had to stop the audio because the narrator read it in a way that distracted from the information the book was trying to convey. This is why you want a professional narrator.

You should never, ever read your own book, even if you are experienced at doing voice-over. Having taken voice-over classes and done some voice-over work myself, I can tell you firsthand that having a "voice" and being able to do an audiobook are not the same thing. For audio to work in a book format, the narrator needs to have some acting experience, because you'll want inflection, emphasis, and drama, even if it's nonfiction. These are things you simply can't get if you choose someone who only has voice-over experience, or just "has a good voice."

You might save some money in the production, but 99.99% of the time it will be a waste of time and effort, and could ultimately negatively affect your book sales. Imagine a bunch of 1- to 3-star reviews on your book page complaining about the narrator. Not a good scenario.

So if you're going to do this, spring for some good talent. Typically, six hours of work are needed to create one hour of audio with a typical audiobook taking about eight to ten hours. Most narrators will charge $300 per finished hour. When you consider how much work is involved to produce a finished book hour (which often requires several retakes), the investment ends up being worth it.

When hiring a narrator, it's important to make sure you like them. If you're doing a series, or have more than one book, you'll want the same narrator for all of them. Consider their voice an aspect of your brand. You'll be surprised to know the number of audiobook listers who have expressed their pet peeve of switching narrators mid-series. Audiobooks create a very personal environment. The listener is inviting the reader into their car, and into their world, and it's important to respect the power of that connection.

Choosing a Sample for Auditions

While Amazon's ACX is the main site for audiobook production/ creation, it's not the only place to list your book. However, let's first look at finding talent. When I spoke to Jason at ACX/Audible about auditions, he shared a few ideas about shopping for talent, and the first thing he emphasizes:

> *"We recommend you keep your audition script to no more than 2-3 pages. You'll typically know right away if the voice is right for your project. You should choose a dynamic selection from your project, rather than the first 2-3 pages, or select 2-3 passages from different sections of your work, to get a sense for the actor's range. "*

Longer scripts can take a ton of studio time, so it's important to keep in mind that the sample will need to be produced. This also means that creating a sample can take quite a bit more time on the part of the narrator than the finished audio (remember: it takes 6 hours of work for 1 hour of finished audio). As Jason mentioned, consider using a sample that's more challenging. You want to find a section that will give you a good sense of the narrator's voice and their ability to do other voices, accents, or characters, if needed. Generally this largely pertains to fiction but even so, your nonfiction book shouldn't be treated as a dull, dry read. So pick the strongest, most impactful section or sections, not the longest. You'll know within two minutes whether that person is right for your book.

Jason at ACX also suggests:

> *Do disclose all the different accents you expect in the book up-front. Don't expect your producer to read your mind; if you don't provide direction on the type of performance you're listening for, your actor will give his or her own interpretation*

of the work. Our philosophy is, the more guidance you provide to your producer—up front—the more satisfied you'll be with the auditions, samples, and finished audiobook production. At minimum, provide a few descriptors of each of the characters included in your audition script, as well as a pronunciation guide for any words that are medical, technical, or conlang (constructed languages, such as Esperanto and Interlingua, or the fictional Dothraki, Na'vi and Klingon languages).

Finding the Right Narrator for Your Book

As I've mentioned, the narration and finding the right voice to do your book are crucially important. To guide you in terms of narration and finding the right person, find inspiration through some of these ideas:

When we were first promoting *The Publicist, Book One*, we helped the author audition and confirm the talent. Ultimately, we hired Lisa Cordileone www.lisacordileone.com) to do *The Publicist, Book One*. She has worked on several audiobooks, and is also a trained actor. Additionally, she's listed on the ACX site as a preferred audiobook reader.

Once Lisa was confirmed, I sent her a blog post the author wrote about the book. www.thepublicistnovel.com/and-the-oscar-goes-to-casting-the-publicist). The blog played on the fact that every author wants their novel to be a movie, and the author built on that a theme, including which actors the author would like to have assigned to the roles. Lisa told me that information actually helped her dig deeper into the characters.

You can apply the same principles with nonfiction by sending the potential voice-over person samples of your work, or links to a video of you speaking. If you have a podcast, invite him or her to listen to an episode or, two. The more you can give backstory, "color," and other information about who you are, the better the narration will be.

Once the book was listed and started to get auditions, I took the extra step of looking at the narrators' backgrounds to see and hear the range of books on their resumes. You can find most of them on Audible, and this information can help you get a real sense of how they would sound doing different aspects of your book. So do your due diligence and really spend as much time as listening to as many samples as you can find.

Most of the narrators do other work, though some are exclusively audio. Most, if not all, will have websites that show previous work, acting background, and other things they are involved in. It's really a good idea to know who you're hiring, since, as we mentioned already, the narrator will be tethered to your entire book series, if you choose to do so. You may want to bring the same narrator in for all your books, regardless of whether or not they're part of a series. If you find someone you work well with, why not continue the relationship? They might even trigger ideas for new new topics and approaches for future books.

When I interviewed Lisa and a few others, I sent them questions via the ACX website to find out how they like to work with authors. Though none of them said so, a red flag might be if any of them say they don't want any contact with the author. While I understand everyone is busy, I think choosing a narrator who is willing to communicate directly with you, the author, and build a connection, is key.

Jason at ACX also recommended taking the time to get in touch with the folks who've auditioned and let them know you appreciate the time they've been willing ot invest. There's a place on the ACX page where you can leave a quick thank you, mentioning that "a quick thank-you goes a long way." I whole-heartedly agree. I actually had a few folks who were auditioning, offer to do additional samples if it would help my decision-making, which I thought was extremely generous.

Male, Female, or Both?

If you've listened to a best-selling book on audio, you may have encountered one or two which use both female and male narrators, having each one read all the narrative and dialogue for their gender. It's not common and is mostly done for fiction and occasionally memoirs. If you're struggling with this idea, keep in mind that it could add a big cost to your bottom line to use both when you really don't need to.

Making the Decision to Hire

The process from start to finish moves along quite quickly. Once you confirm who you want to hire, you'll make them an offer, and then give them a chance to respond and accept it. From there, all communication will be between you (the author) and the narrator.

They'll record a 15-minute session and upload it to ACX for your approval. Where Lisa went several steps beyond expected in order to narrate the best book she could. First, she asked for the entire book right off the bat so she could read it through, and second, she took the time to highlight difficult names so she could double-check their pronunciation. Just through these seemingly simple things, what was critically shown was how hiring a true professional can only enhance the accuracy and professionalism of your audiobook.

Once you approve the 15-minute sample, the actual recording process will begin. Keep in mind that you'll define the dates for production. Tell the narrator how much time they have. We gave Lisa well over a month to which she finished in a couple of weeks. Most narrators will tell you right off the bat when they can start so there are no misunderstandings around timing.

Deciding If You Want to Go Exclusive

So should you go exclusive with ACX? While the royalties may be higher, it may not make sense to sign over all your book sales rights for seven years which is the duration of their exclusivity. Once you go exclusive, you're kind of stuck, and new audiobook sites are popping up all the time. While a lot of people do default to Audible, because of Amazon, these other audiobook sites are offering supremely great deals to get new customers:

Audiobooks.com is a great example. They have a great selection of titles, a thirty-day free trial, and their monthly membership rates are slightly lower than Audible. Audible is, however, adding in more free stuff for users who are also part of the Prime membership. They know the competition is growing out there for audiobooks.

If you choose to have your book listed on Audiobooks.com, you first have to sign up with Author's Republic (www.authorsrepublic.com). If you let Author's Republic sell through all channels, your book will be featured on sites like audiobooksnow.com, talkingbookz.com, and about twenty others, not to mention Audible/Amazon.

Ultimately, audiobooks make a great companion to your print or e-book, so consider this as a potential component for your launch, or perhaps do the audiobook after your book has been launched. I know a lot of authors who often do different "editions" of their book, which is then considered a new release and keeps the book, and publication date, fresh. However, it can annoy readers who end up buying your book twice, especially if the content hasn't changed a lot, so keep that in mind.

Powerful Podcasting

Many authors, and especially non-fiction authors, will start a podcast around their book, instead of doing an audiobook, by creating audio soundbytes using services like SoundCloud and others.

If you decide to do a podcast, remember this isn't just a place to share audio content about your book. Use it to share more than that.

It can be informative commentary, or you can invite other industry experts for a discussion, but a podcast is not your chance to read from your book. It doesn't work. There are so many lively and informative podcasts out there. If you decide to step into audio content using a podcast, explore other, similar podcasts first, so you have a good sense of what's currently out there. Know who is competing for your target audience's time and attention.

Deciding to Self-Publish

"A journey of a thousand miles begins with a single step."
– Confucius

Since I first started talking about print on demand publishing in 2000, many changes have occurred in the self-publishing industry. Many of the companies that once were thriving are now part of a bigger publishing model. iUniverse, for example, used to be a large entity on its own. After being bought out by AuthorHouse, they formed Author Solutions.

Due to the sheer number of self-publishing companies out their vying for your book, selecting the right company will be your most crucial decision.

This is a very fluid industry, and publishers are constantly evolving and forming new conglomerates and partnerships. When I first used this route to publish some thirteen years ago, things were very different. While the market has stablized a bit recently, you still need to be careful. Do your homework before selecting your publisher.

The Future of Self-Publishing

In 2015, Authorearnings.com released a statistic stating that 40% of all e-book author earnings generated on Amazon were indie published. As of the printing of this book, approximately 4,500 books are published every single day in the U.S., and 80% of them are self-published. This number does not even include some of the books published solely e-books, which are untrackable, as many of them are published without an ISBN number. Amazon has said they have around four billion e-book titles currently listed across all their stores internationally.

Much of the flood of print book content has happened because of the print on demand option, which is, as the name implies, an on-demand way of printing books that many authors have gravitated to. But with so many titles, not all of them can be viably competitive. Around 1% of everything that's self-published is considered to meet "industry editorial standards". These "standards" are applied by reviewers and bookstores alike. If your book doesn't meet those industry standards, it will likely never be able to meet your sales goals either.

The other element that has led to the surge of self-published titles is the many high-profile business people who have chosen to go this route. We worked with Guy Kawasaki, who is most known for his best-selling book called *Enchantment*. He eventually turned down a six-figure publishing deal to self-publish his latest book, *APE: Author, Publisher, Entrepreneur*.

Another unique variation to the self-publishing world, are authors choosing to be "hybrids" (both traditionally and self-published). In this type of model, books start in the self-published world and later, crosses over, bringing new light and new life to the indie market. *Fifty Shades of Grey* was originally self-published, and later picked up by a major publishing house.

Nitty Gritty Time

Let's get down to the details you should evalute.

First of all, it's important to note that book prices vary considerably, depending on the length of the book. The reality of self-publishing is that print on demand books are slightly more expensive to produce. To offset the higher print on demand printing cost, the author's "cut" will be slightly less than if you did a traditional print run (also called offset printing).

As a first-time author, you have to be careful not to produce a book that is priced out of your market. While the printing process has become more efficient and costs have come down, you could still make as much as $1 less per book. Depending on the length of your book, you may even be looking at a difference greater than that. We talk about about pricing later in this book and what I've found to be most effective.

Another thing to keep in mind while reviewing publishers is whether or not they list with Ingram[1] or similar site. My personal experience with listing my titles with Ingram as well as Baker and Taylor, is that it helped boost sales. Why is this important to consider? Many of the bookstores I spoke with will only stock a book if it's listed on Ingram or Baker and Taylor.

Some publishers are vehemently opposed to listing with either of those companies. A big reason being that they don't want to fork over the percentage Ingram demands in exchange for a coveted listing in its catalog. Some publishers give you the option of submitting the listing yourself if you get your own ISBN, which means you are the publisher of record. Depending on what you decide to be your primary sales venue of your book, having to consider a listing service or not will rank differently in priority. Weigh your options and see what will most benefit you and your book sales.

A third option is listing with Books in Print (www.booksinprint.com). Books in Print is a database of books available for purchase. If you opted not to list with Ingram, some brick and mortar store may consider stocking your book as long as you have a listing with Books in Print.

Hiring the Right Self-Publisher for You

We've discussed self-publishing and familiarized you with the terminology. Let's look at the details that will matter to your book specifically, and help you work out which publisher is right for you.

Asking good questions is fundamental. Do your due diligence. You want to know that you're going with a publisher who will not only do

---

[1] Ingram is one of the largest book wholesalers in the United States. Its database of books is linked to most bookstores around the country.

a good job for you, but is stable, and won't end up going out of business the minute your book is published.

Selecting which publisher you end up with will usually depend on your book's content. If your book is going to have colored interiors, you're going to need to find a publisher who can accommodate color printing. Though most of them do provide that option, know that the quality can vary from publisher to publisher. Do you have a book with lots of tables, graphics, or clip art? Find a company that can handle them, and won't charge you an arm and a leg to convert the files into digital formats. Discuss these kinds of needs and their costs up front instead of letting them end up being an expensive surprise later on.

The other factor to consider is whether you'll be doing any bulk orders, whether it is for clients or even speaking events. If you need books in bulk, you'll want to ask the publisher if they can accommodate this via an offset print run. In high enough quantities, it would save you money. How much money you save will depend on the page count of your book, but I've seen bulk orders of 500 to 8,000 shave off between $2 and $3 per book. That is money you can put back in your pocket. In many cases, once you have the book file (PDF and the final cover) you can find a printer who does offset, and you don't have to stick with your publisher. Publishers will often discourage this but most won't prevent you from doing it, unless it is specifically mentioned in your contract. If bulk orders is something you'll need on a regular basis, and the publisher you are inquiring with does refuse, you would need to consider using a different publisher.

Once you determine the precise technical requirements of your book, it's time to formulate the criteria for your "ideal" publisher. After you have narrowed your selection to three or four publishers, take a closer look at their websites, preview their contracts, get a sense of how they operate, and how accommodating and knowledgeable their representatives are.

While much of your communication with your publisher is encouraged via e-mail, don't be afraid to contact them by phone. Something I do when researching self-publishing companies is call their customer service departments five or six different times and ask them the same question. If you get a consistent answer, then you know you're dealing with a company that effectively trains and communicates with its staff. If you get a different answer every time you call, you should probably look elsewhere. Why does this matter? If a company doesn't make sure its customer service staff is always up to par, consider what could happen if the next caller was a customer interested in buying your book. How confident is your reader going to be about you and your work?

How Healthy Is Your Publisher?

There are some savvy ways to determine the health and viability of the publisher you're about to sign with. Here are a few you might want to consider:

See what others are saying about them. If you can't find any online dialogue, then see if you can reach out to a few authors who have published through them. You can do this by doing a quick Google search on the authors. Smart authors will most likely have websites that will let you know how to get in touch with them.

Advertising will tell the real story. Every publisher will seem to be offering the best deal in town. If there's too much misleading copy on the website, consider it a red flag and move on. Misleading ads might be a sign of issues that have yet to surface.

Other factors I use to determine whether a company is right for me is its website, and how user-friendly its ordering process is. Most (if not all) of these self-publishing companies will have bookstores on their websites of their various titles. Take the time to order a book from their websites. This will accomplish quite a few things: You'll see firsthand if the company's delivery promises are kept. You'll also be able to examine the product. What is the print quality like? Is the binding secure? You're paying for this product, so it helps to see what the end result is. Last, but certainly not least, keep in mind that someday, a new reader might be trying to order one of your books. It will be important for them to have a good experience.

Check Your Contract Carefully

Once you've narrowed down your list of publishers, the next thing you want to do is to review the contract carefully. Know exactly what is and isn't included in your agreement. Before you sign any contract, review the points listed below to make sure you understand what you are and aren't getting.

Keep in mind that typically you'll need to have completed the signed contract and paid the publishing fee by the time you upload your files for printing.

1. Rights: Be absolutely certain you retain all rights to your book. "All rights" means all of the rights—including, but not limited to, foreign, film, audio, hardcover/paperback books, and electronics. Be positive you are only granting revocable permission for a self-publishing company publisher to produce and distribute your book as orders are received. Make sure that it's a nonexclusive publishing agreement. If the publisher you are considering requires you to assign any right to the publisher for a specific period of time, be sure to ask what they are going to do in exchange for this time constraint as well as how such an assignment would benefit you.

2. Copyright: It is in your best interest for you to personally fill out and sign the forms, pay the filing fee, and file for your copyright protection with the Library of Congress. By doing so, you know,

without a doubt, that the copyright is in your name. Once your copyright is recorded and granted, you will receive the certificate of copyright to retain.

3. Fair usage: Be prepared to provide your publisher with copies of correspondence granting permission for any copyright-protected material you have included in your book.

4. Cancellation: Look for a hassle-free termination clause in the agreement that allows you to withdraw from the publishing arrangement upon written notice (an acknowledged e-mail should be acceptable), and to have your book immediately removed from the system and its online bookstore.

5. Nonexclusive: This means that, in addition to your publisher, you're able to publish your book through other methods—including another self-publishing company. The nonexclusive provision is most handy to have when you're making a transition between publishers, or perhaps issuing a revised edition. The nonexclusive provision is another way to keep your options open. Having two books that are the same with the exception of the ISBN—which identifies the publisher—could create confusion when booksellers try to order your book and not advised.

6. Control: You must understand which party will have final say over which aspect of your book. Certain book production requirements are fixed and can't be changed. Production requirements such as the minimum and maximum number of pages, the page size, paper weight, and the minimum width of margins would all fall under this category. If the company provides the service of formatting your book for you, be sure you know if you have any recourse other than simply accepting what they have done. Some of these companies use a fixed-template format that won't allow any deviations, and others are flexible and will work with your formatting as long as you follow their guidelines. Factor

in any surcharges that could apply to formatting your book the way you want.

7. Editing and proofreading: The final editing and proofreading of your book is your responsibility. Self-publishing companies are *not responsible* for editing or proofreading your book. In fact, most of these publishers will not change a single word in your book without your written instructions to make the change.

8. Graphics: With some companies, there could be a surcharge for illustrations, charts, tables, footnotes, and photographs. If your book has a lot of graphics, request a written quote for any additional charges that might apply.

9. Formatting: Most self-publishing companies will have formatting guidelines for how you must prepare your book file in terms of page size and margins. Be sure to follow the instructions, and call your publisher's representative if you have any questions. An improperly formatted book will create problems during the conversion process.

10. Production time: This could vary from a few short weeks to many long months of waiting until your book is available for sale. How long it takes often depends on the condition of the book file you've prepared, the workload of the publisher's production department, and whether they do the conversion in-house or farm it out to a third party. Be sure you have a firm understanding regarding when you'll receive the first proof copies of your book.

11. Proofing correction costs: Usually, the setup charges include making a certain number of changes as part of the proofing process. Inquire whether or not additional corrections to the proof copy over the agreed-upon number of changes would incur a surcharge.

12. Corrections after approval: Remember to find out up front what the cost is to correct typos after your book has been approved. Some

companies will correct a few typos at no charge. Others will charge a flat fee regardless of how minor the change might be. Some may allow it after a book has been added to their system. Others may not be so willing.

13. Revised editions: There could come a time when you need to do a major revision or update of time-critical material in your self-published book. Be sure to ask the companies you're considering what their policies and charges are for swapping book files to produce a revised edition of your book. The fee should be considerably less than their initial setup fee, as there's usually less work involved. Usually, a second edition with significantly new material will require a new ISBN and perhaps another copyright filing. "Significantly new material" is usually defined as approximately 15 to 20 percent of the book being reworked with new material.

14. Royalties: Be absolutely certain you understand how your earned royalties are calculated. Some self-publishing companies pay authors a percentage based on the selling price of the book. The percentage is higher on retail sales placed directly through the publisher's online bookstore than the percentage on wholesale orders placed by book-sellers. Be sure to understand how much expenses will be accounted for as well as what expense items are included and not. Expenses can include shipping, expedited printing, or anything else related to the production of the physical book. Ask if expenses are likely to increase in the foreseeable future. This is important because when an increase in expenses occurs, your royalty percentage will stay the same. Your royalty earnings will decrease because the net selling price debits the expenses.

15. Assignment of royalties: Some companies will allow an author to assign royalties to a third party, who will then benefit from book sales. Such assignments of royalties can be essential especially if the book is the product of a group effort. Find out if they accept a pre-assignment

of royalties to a spouse, offspring, relative, or close friend in the event of an author's death. This will allow the book to continue to be published and to pay royalties.

16. Confidential information: Be sure you have an understanding of the publisher's privacy policies. Authors need to be sure that if they publish under a pseudonym, their true identities will be kept private.

17. Returns: Most self-publishing companies will not accept books returned by booksellers. But one of the many advantages of self-publishing is that books are only produced in the quantities needed to fill orders. If your publisher is factoring returns into the selling and distribution equation, be sure you understand what's involved. Usually, royalties are not paid on books as long as they are subject to being returned to the publisher for full credit. If your self-publishing company accepts returns, ask who bears the expense of producing these unsold books, and how long booksellers have to return them. Frequently, when books are returned, they are so damaged from being handled that they can't be used to fill another order. You need to determine if entering into an agreement with a self-publishing company that accepts returns is worth the uncertainty of not knowing what has actually been sold and what is more or less out on consignment.

18. Author book purchases: Some companies will sell an author's book to the author at a special discount—but with some publishers, the author's discount is about 20 percent, which isn't as good as the standard 40 percent wholesale discount extended to booksellers. A few publishers pay royalties on all purchases of the author's book, even when authors buy their own books at the wholesale price. Ask who pays the shipping charges when authors order 20 or more copies of their books.

19. Order delivery time: Most self-publishing companies will ship all book orders within 24 to 48 hours. Confirm what the usual time frame

is to process and fill an order for your book. Nothing will turn off a customer more than having to wait weeks to receive a self-published book that they rightfully expect to arrive at their door only a few days after they've placed the order. Prompt order processing and accurate fulfillment are essential for keeping customers happy, and building repeat business and word-of-mouth sales.

20. Annual maintenance and listing fees: Some publishers charge annual fees to maintain your book in their system, or to keep your book listed in their online bookstores, often in addition to the fees imposed by distributors. You are obligated to pay these imposed ongoing costs, even if you haven't sold enough books to cover the charge. Unfortunately, not selling enough books to cover these continuing costs is a potential risk. Failure to pay will result in having your book (which you thought would never go out of print) pulled from the publisher's inventory, unless you come up with the money to maintain your book's presence in its online bookstore. If Lightning Source is involved, your book will be purged from its system, and from Ingram distribution as well, for nonpayment of fees. What these fees provide for the publishers is a way to produce an ongoing cash flow even if your book doesn't sell—or only sells a few copies each month. They're hedging their bet to generate income from your book regardless of what you do, or don't do, to promote your book. Make it a point to ask if you'll be expected to pay these fees, which are usually required in advance. I'm not a fan of these listing fees, and find that most reputable publishers did away with them long ago.

21. Thresholds: A few self-publishing companies are implementing the concept of threshold achievements for authors. When an author's book has sold a certain number of copies, those accumulated sales demonstrate the marketability of the book. Because of the encouraging book orders, several things can happen to further benefit an author:

for example, the percentage of royalty could increase, or the author will qualify to participate in co-op advertising sponsored in part by the publisher, and/or increased efforts are made by the publisher to gain more exposure for the book.

22. Guaranteed delivery: When you have to fly somewhere to do a public speaking engagement where you're able to sell your book, you need to be sure you have books to sell. These days you don't need the additional hassle of packing books in your luggage; just find out if your publisher will ship your books directly to the hotel and guarantee the delivery will arrive before you check in. A few publishers will pay normal ground shipping charges when you order twenty or more books. Check with your publisher to find out the lead time required for your books to be delivered on time to a third-party location.

23. Transitional services: Even high-speed digital presses can reach the point when demand for a book exceeds a publisher's production capabilities. When keeping up with an increasing flow of orders ceases to be cost-effective, you need a self-publishing company that can arrange a print run on an offset press. You might want to amend your agreement to allow your publisher to make these arrangements on your behalf and continue to publish under the house name of your publisher, or require your publisher to give you assistance if you exercise your option to make your own preparations for a commercial print run. If a traditional publisher makes you an offer, you need a publisher who is able and willing to work with you, and is contracted to help you through this transitional period by keeping your book available until your traditionally published book is released.

24. Redundant backups: Paramount to the effective operations of every self-publishing company are safeguarding the author's book files, which are used by their system to produce books. These vital files are their inventory. Without the files, there's nothing to sell. Redundant backup files are constantly being created to ensure the publisher's

ability to maintain a virtually interruption-free operation. In our instant gratification-seeking society, unforeseen delays can be devastating to a publisher's ability to continue to do business.

25. Policy changes: Be sure to ask about how and when authors will be notified of future policy changes that could affect your book and the agreement you have entered into with the self-publishing company. Some changes that provide additional benefits to authors are made retroactively so both a publisher's current and new authors can benefit from new policies. This can be good or bad, depending on the situation. Watch out if your publisher tries to charge you for services rendered retroactively. Don't pay—instead, take a close look at your publishing agreement, and give serious consideration to exercising your right to terminate your relationship with them at once.

And Now...Your Book and Its Cover

Once you've made your final selection, signed the contract, and paid the publishing fee, it's time for the submission process. Most of the submissions are done via the publisher's website, and there are myriad places to get your questions answered.

And there's more involved than simply uploading your manuscript: you have to also consider what will appear on your cover, such as your author bio and a blurb/sales pitch about the book itself.

While you're struggling with the nit-picky details of this stage, consider this: Every bit of information you submit will somehow, somewhere, end up in your book. So take your time.

Visit a bookstore and examine books on your subject. They should give you plenty of ideas about what works for things like your author bio, back cover information (your sales pitch for the book), back flap information (if you are going with a hardcover), quotes from satisfied customers or other authors, and so on. Don't copy, but learn. Learn from the pros—the authors who have gone before you. When you've familiarized yourself with all of these aspects, fire up that computer and begin your publishing process.

When you're ready, you can upload your manuscript/book file (or send it to them via the U.S. Postal Service or another shipping service), and submit all the pertinent information. When you fill out the forms, it's incredibly important for you to be very thorough. Dot your i's and cross all your t's, leave nothing blank, and polish and finalize everything, including pesky things like your author bio and back cover/flap information (see the section about editors for help with this).

Something to think about:

The following books were self-published:

A Christmas Carol by Charles Dickens
Adventures of Huckleberry Finn by Mark Twain
What Color Is Your Parachute? by Richard N. Bolles
*The One Minute Manage*r by Kenneth Blanchard, PhD, and Spencer Johnson, MD
In Search of Excellence by Thomas J. Peters & Robert H. Waterman, Jr.
The Toilet Paper Entrepreneur: The tell-it-like-it-is guide to cleaning up in business, even if you are at the end of your roll by Mike Michalowicz
Life's Little Instruction Book by H. Jackson Brown, Jr.
The Christmas Box by Richard Paul Evans
The Celestine Prophecy by James Redfield
Fifty Shades of Grey by E. L. James

How Much Self-Promotion Should You Be Doing, Really?

When it comes to self-promotion, most of us fall a bit flat. We have high hopes, but then something happens. Generally, we just get busy, or distracted or, we simply feel like it's too big a mountain for us to climb. When you have a big goal like "self-promotion," try breaking it down into manageable pieces. Let's face it, unless you have superpowers, most of us can't spend all day every day promoting. But can you do one thing each day? Consider giving yourself a target of between 1-5 promotional tasks per day. It doesn't matter what they are. It could be as simple as sending a thank you-note, or as involved as scheduling some tweets to post. You don't have to do everything at once, or be the master-of-all-promoters. Just do one thing at a time. You'll be amazed how much progress you can make.

How a Publisher Can Kill Your Success

"There are no secrets to success. It is the result of preparation, hard work, and learning from failure."
– Colin Powell

When it comes to publishing, you have more options than ever to get your book out there. By definition, however, self-publishing means you are your own publisher, whether or not you use an ISBN from a self-publishing house.

The reason I mention this is because you retain all control over the book: creative, digital, and international. Some publishers, however, don't seem to agree with many of the standards that are out there and create systems that make it difficult for authors to sell books.

I've recently had an influx of authors saddled with bad deals from indie publishers, with problems running the gamut from not having access to or control of their e-book, to being forced to buy marketing programs that not only don't move the needle, but have also negatively impacted their book. Serious stuff!

If you aren't sure what to look for with regard to your publisher, here are a few things that are, in my view, musts for a book to be successful:

Pricing

You must always be able to control pricing. Bottom line. If your publisher is telling you you need to price your book at X because of their print costs, that's one thing, but you should fully understand what their internal costs are before you choose your publisher. We had an author recently who was told by her publisher that she had to price her e-book at $20. In most cases, a digital book will sell better than the print book, but at $20, you'd be lucky to get one sale. You need to ask before signing with a publisher how pricing is determined. Even with companies like Createspace, they suggest a price to you, and if you want to go lower than that suggested price, they'll tell you why that's a bad idea, but it's generally your choice if you don't mind reducing your per-book profits. As I said, most publishers will offer guidance, but publishers who insist on a certain price or, even worse, set it for you, could have a serious negative impact on your book's success.

E-book Flexibility

If your publisher is creating your e-book file for you, it's always good to get file/digital copies for your files. You'll want to ask for it in different formats (such as: ePub, Mobi, PDF), and if they won't release them to you, ask them why. We had an author who could not get access to her e-book. She could not gift the e-book file or give it away to reviewers (which would save her a lot of time and money over the expense of buying and shipping books). She literally had her hands tied. They also didn't allow her to change her e-book pricing, which is a big part of a successful launch strategy. E-book price points, sales, and free days are fantastic ways to gain more traction for your book.

Publisher Discounts

Before you sign with a publisher, be sure to ask them how much author copies will cost you. Most reputable self-publishing companies have this outlined so there is no guessing, and those who don't have this information at the ready are questionable.

Book Updates

If you need to update your book, what happens? Maybe you don't fall into this category, but I sure do. My books *Red Hot Internet Publicity* and *How to Sell Books by the Truckload* need constant updates. Do you know how your publisher handles this? One author we work with had actually updated her book and sent it to the publisher with an updated copyright date. They loaded it onto Amazon with the old date, and when she asked why, she was told that they could not update the Amazon information to match the new book copyright date until she sold X number of books. I was floored and told her it was a scam and to contact Amazon and tell them what was happening. If you have a book that requires frequent updates, ask about your publisher's policies before you sign, and get it in writing.

E-book Promotions

While to some degree this falls under the e-book pricing and flexibility, it's still worth mentioning that some publishers will not let you do discounts or freebie book promotions on Amazon. Trust me when I say you will want to do these kinds of promotions, so ask them what their policy is and, again, get it in writing.

Amazon Listing

Who has access to your Amazon listing? Unless you're with a traditional publishing house, you should have full access to this, no question. Not having access to this listing can be really problematic if you're trying to update your book description with a blurb or endorsement, or change it in some other way.

Marketing

First, let me say that this isn't a sales pitch to hire us—at all—but if you're going to outsource your marketing to anyone, very seriously consider the value of the marketing programs an indie publisher is offering you. Yes, some can be good, but many are not. I recently worked with an author who bought $15,000 worth of social media marketing, which amounted to a few Facebook updates, a Twitter background, a few tweets, and that was about it. Don't fall for the hype! Ask for details.

The other thing we've seen, are publishers who present lists of journalists and bloggers who will be be "blasted with your message." Let's say they promise 250,000 journalists and 500 bloggers. Sounds impressive, right? From that type of pitching, which is essentially just bcc'ing everyone in a single email, with no custom pitch and no email personalization, guess what kind of response they get? Yes, crickets.

Websites

Many publishers will offer to do websites for you, and, while you can find great deals, you want to be sure you can actually access these sites after they are up. Often the publisher retains all control and does all your updates, so, while the site itself might have only cost you $300, the updates are very expensive. We actually had an author who walked away from her site because the publisher never kept it up-to-date and never returned her calls. If you're considering an offer to do your website, find out what their cost is for updates and what your access is. You'll need access to the control panel at a minimum.

It's On You

The responsibility for finding a good publisher is on you, the author, so ask good questions. If you don't know, or aren't sure—ask, don't assume. Finding a good indie publisher can really help your book succeed, but finding a bad one could kill any chance for your book's success. After working for so long, and investing so much energy and effort into your book, why would you risk making a choice that could kill it before it even has a chance to soar?

Becoming Your Own Publisher

"I have always believed that writing advertisements is the second most profitable form of writing. The first, of course, is ransom notes..."
– Philip Dusenberry

If you decide to become a publisher yourself rather than using a print on demand company, you may need to do a few things to ready your new publishing company before you launch any books. This of course depends on whether you'll run the company under your business, or as a division of your business. Here are some of items to consider:

Becoming a Business: Regardless of how you publish, you should check to see if you need to get a separate business license. If you become your own publishing house, look into your options, and decide whether to incorporate, form an LLC, or remain a sole proprietor. Talk to an accountant or CPA, as well as a lawyer you trust, to find out which option is best for you. If you just publish under your business, you likely won't need to do any of this separately. You can simply brand the book to your business and call it day. But if you think you'll be publishing more than one book, it might make sense to carefully consider how you'll present this and future books to the world.

Naming Your Publishing Company: Now you need to give your publishing company a name. What will you call it? Think about where you plan to go with you venture into publishing. If you decided not to self-publish, you are probably going to be publishing more than one book. What will the other books look like? Do you plan to publish a series? Do you plan to publish other authors? All of these possibilities should be considered.

Branding/Logo: Branding is so important and often it's something we don't think of until after we launch. I encourage you to think about what you want your publishing brand to look like, and how closely it will be tied to your business brand. We will discuss branding more in depth in a later chapter, but for now, know that you'll need to understand exactly what you want your image in the world to be. Knowing how you want to "show up" in the publishing world is often crucial to your future success.

It's Not About You

Me, me, me: many companies push themselves too much in social media, or any kind of online promotion. When I've consulted with business owners, I'll often encourage them to share first and ask later. A company's percentage of shares should always be bigger than their percentage of asks. What I mean by this is, they need to spend most of their social media time sharing ideas or cost-saving tips (everyone loves those). By becoming a resource, you will build a much stronger following. es, you can still make them an offer like 20% off, for example, but people will be more inclined to respond if you're not bombarding them with sales pitches all the time.

Your Self-Publishing Checklist

The road to ignorance is paved with good editors.
– George Bernard Shaw

When it comes to getting a book to market, there's a lot to do and remember. Here's a checklist that covers many of the things you'll want to remember and take care of!

_____ **Establish a production budget:** Contact and get bids from all subcontractors; account for variables, such as author photo, cover photo or illustration, permissions, and seller's permit; add fixed costs: ISBN log book, bar code, copyright, and so on.

_____**Establish a marketing budget:** How much will you spend on marketing? What will you outsource? Now is a great time to start gathering that data.

_____ **Edit:** Copyeditors check grammar, punctuation, spelling, usage, logic and flow. *The Writing Right* chapter goes into more detail as to why you need solid editing.

_____**Printers and printing options:** Find printers and determine your printing options.

_____**ISBN:** Buy a block of ISBNs from R.R. Bowker at www.isbn.org/standards/home/isbn/us/application.asp

____**Copyright:** Send two copies of the printed book with the copyright fee to the Library of Congress Copyright Office. Download forms from www.loc.gov/copyright/forms.

____**List your book on "Books In Print":** R.R. Bowker's website at www.Bowkerlink.com

____**Publishers:** Will you go indie for this project? If so, identify which self-publishing company you will use.

____ **Secure permissions:** Get signed consent and release from all necessary sources, including for quotations, graphics, and photos.

____ **Have your author photo taken:** Have a professional photographer take a "head shot" for inclusion on the cover of your book, and have your photographer also create files for the cover and website designers, per their specifications.

____ **Write jacket copy and author bio:** For this important piece, I suggest getting some feedback from people who know marketing, having your content editor check it, or hiring someone to write these two pieces for you. We're often too close to our own message, and the cover/book jacket copy, especially, is critical. If done well, your cover copy, or "blurb," can significantly help your book marketing. If done poorly...well, not so much.

____ **Secure endorsements:** Send copyedited manuscripts labeled "uncorrected copy" to people of influence and request brief comments or reviews; and get signed consent and release forms from all contributors.

____ **Layout/production:** The graphic designer creates a look for the book, lays it out, and coordinates with the proofer.

_____ **Confirm printing cost:** The designer gives actual page count and cover specifications to the printing company, and delivers any revised pricing.

_____ **Establish book price:** Once you know page count, you should be able to establish a price for your book. You should also look at competing titles, because in some categories books may be priced higher or lower than you might expect, depending on the market. For example, finance books (targeted specifically to financial officers) will often have a much higher price, so it's good to know what is standard in your market. A lot of this research can be done on Amazon.com.

_____ **Get bar code:** You can obtain one with price/ISBN embedded ($20-50): Ask for a Bookland EAN/13 with add-on/price extension (available from many vendors; see www.isbn.org for a listing).

_____ **Proof:** The proofreader and author read "galleys" prior to printing to eliminate any remaining or introduced errors.

_____ **Get CIP (Library of Congress Cataloging in Publication data):** If your book is eligible for the program (see guidelines and all other application links at pcn.loc.gov/pcn), click on "To Join," and complete the publisher application. After you are assigned an account number and password, return to the site and click on "Account Number," enter your number and password, and complete a Preassigned Control Number Application.

_____ **Print:** The designer sends the electronic file to printer.

_____ **Register fictitious business name:** Do this if necessary.

_____ **Get seller's permit:** Obtain this from your County Franchise Tax Board.

_____ **Register title with Bowker:** Include your title in the R. R. Bowker directories, so product information is available to major retailers, librarians, and independent booksellers across the country. Register at www.bowkerlink.com.

Determining the Best
Time to Publish

"There ain't nothing that breaks up homes, country and nations like somebody publishing their memoirs."
– Will Rogers

Often, your book's launch date is determined by one simple factor: the book is finally done.

When you launch your book is perhaps the most important element in the life of your tome. Giving your book a solid start date and start plan is crucial. Though in keeping with the idea that your book is your business card, you would apply the same principles to the book that you did for your business.

With this comes another decision. Do you want this book to be commercially successful, just an extension of your business, or both? Neither answer is wrong nor right. It really comes down to what's right for your business which will affect your timing.

Commercial or Not?

If you want your book to compete commercially instead of simply being a brand extension, you'll have to devote ten times the amount of marketing and attention to it. My books are all brand extensions. I know my limitations and my focus, which is my business. My books are stepping stones to getting more business, and all the other things we talked about earlier in the book.

But as you dig into the idea of creating a book, other things may pop up for you. You may have a yet-unrealized desire to see your book hit a best-seller list, or you may wish to be interviewed on national television. This isn't to say this can't happen, even if never intended your book to be a commercial success. Sometimes publishing "magic" kicks in and those things happen anyway. That's a high-quality problem to have.

For now, however, you should decide up front how well-known you want the book to be. This will save you a lot of time as you plan your book rollout.

How do you know which goal is right for you? Most of us probably know the answer from the start, but if you don't, here's a thought. In order to compete commercially, you would require 90% of whatever time you have allocated for marketing, planning and strategy. A book that's going to be a brand extension? Probably only 50%. That's still a lot, but the brand extension model leaves you with room to breathe and run your business. Depending on your goals for the book, you should seek publicity opportunities like reviews and media, but in a much smaller way than you would if you were going for the national spotlight.

Timing and Book Release

Before you can determine your start date, you need to figure out best time to release your book. If you're interested in gaining national media attention for your book, or doing some sort of major launch for it, when you release your book can make a big difference. Again, this all comes down to the goals you have for your book.

At the same time, you may want to look at busy times for your business and capitalize on that. For those where busy times aren't always predicatable, plan your launch just before that time hits.

For my business, it varies from year to year, but because so much of what we do is driven by the national publishing market, I do find that August tends to be slower. It is typically the slowest month in publishing, mostly because so many New Yorkers are gone in August.

If you have a seasonal business, like tax preparation, or something else that's driven by a particular time of year, you may want to consider doing a release a few months prior to that season. Why so early? Because if you're sending review copies to publications, or trying to get interviews, or speaking engagements, most of these places will need some advance notice. Starting early is always a good idea.

If you want to avoid the majority of the competition, try releasing your book during an off-season. For example, publishers used to release books in three seasons: winter, summer and fall. Now the main season for publishing seems to be fall, thereby capturing their share of the holiday market. It's not that you can't release a book around this time, but know that you will likely be competing with many major titles. This, however, might not always be the case, and that's where some additional sleuthing can come in handy.

While there are a variety of ways to track what publishers will be releasing, there is one resource that I find most current: Publisher's Marketplace (www.publishersmarketplace.com). This site serves up a daily newsletter called *Publishers Lunch*, and a weekly newsletter called *Deal Lunch* (where they share all the deals signed the previous week). I would recommend joining this site as soon as you can, so you can track who is doing what, who's buying, and what's being released. The service is free, but for $20 a month you can get access to a bunch of back-end data, a treasure trove of publishing data, such as editorial staff, all deals for the past twelve months (or more), and anything else related to publishing and book releases. Even if New York publishers aren't of interest to you, you still play in the same sandbox, and information is power. Arm yourself well.

The next piece to figuring out your release date is something I recommend that you do on an ongoing basis: monitor the competition. Who else is in your market, and what are they doing? Are you on their mailing lists? If you're not, you should be. Keep an eye on what other business authors in your market are doing; especially the leaders in your industry. This will also give you some idea of what else is happening in your market. If you plan to be successful, you should never operate in a vacuum.

The final piece to figuring out your release date are news items. Are you staying on top of everything related to your industry? This will not only benefit you as you determine the best publishing season for your book, but it will also help you understand new trends in your industry (and possibly incorporate them into your book). It will also give you the opportunity to start looking at (yes, now) market trends and hot industry topics.

Marketing, even in its pre-release phase, is all about joining the conversation. To be successful in that conversation, you must keep up with what's happening. Tracking is pretty easy these days with sites like Mention (www.mention.net/) and Talkwalker (www.talkwalker.com/en). Just plug in your desired keywords, and voila! Results will start appearing in your inbox shortly. Also, if you're already "out there," be sure to get an alert service on your name too. That way you can make sure you know who's saying what, and where your name and/or business name are appearing.

Keeping Tabs Online

With so much social media buzz going on out there, online reputation management has become important. For years, Google Alerts has been great for keeping track of what's being said about you online. But Google plans to discontinue it gradually, and several other players have come in as solid competitors to the online monitoring world. Here are some additional online reputation management tools. They're a great way to keep track of what's being said about you, your book and/or product online:

Addict-o-matic: When I first logged on here, I was surprised how much information was out there about me that Google Alerts didn't pick up. Addict-o-matic is a free service, and a great resource. My only complaint is they don't have an RSS feed that I can subscribe to in order to keep me posted with weekly or even daily additions. Hopefully that will come soon. For now, here's the link: www.addictomatic.com/. The best part about this service is that it doesn't require that I sign in or sign up for anything. I like that. I have way too many subscriptions and passwords I can't remember as it is.

Trackur.com: This site claims to be Google Alerts on steroids. The service is quite thorough and outstanding, and while it's not a free service, they do offer a free trial. Give it a shot and see what you think.

Keyhole.com: This is a search for hashtags and social media mentions, URLs, and keywords, and provides analytics of those searches. Costs about $116/month.

BookScan Numbers Don't Lie, and Neither Should You

It's fine when your Uncle Harry comes back from a fishing trip with "fish stories," but don't try telling any of those in publishing. What do I mean by fish stories? I mean inflating your sales numbers. Don't do it. Why? Because Nielsen's BookScan has your number. Literally. Anyone in the industry (even literary agents) can check these numbers to see if your sales figures add up. So leave the fish tales for the fish, and don't fiddle with book sales numbers. Because, unlike your Uncle Harry's catch of the day, someone is bound to find out. The good news? Once your book is on Amazon, you can easily gain access to your numbers via your Author Central page.

Branding: The Secret to Selling More Books

"Well-managed brands live on—only bad brand managers die."
– George Bull

If you've ever wondered what motivates people to buy a book, consider this: consumers don't buy a book, they buy a brand or, as a friend of mine says, they crave a brand.

This is true now more than ever. Why? Because people want consistency, value, as well as wanting to be entertained, enlightened, or educated. A brand, when done properly, can pull in readers to your site, your message, and your book. Though branding for your business might not be a new concept, when it comes to a book, it might feel like you're getting into unknown territory. Branding for a book is much like that for a business. In fact, if you love your business brand, it might be a great idea to extend it to your book. If you aren't sure that you've defined your brand well enough, and are looking to your book to do that for you, that's possible, too. Here's how to do it.

Brands, in their traditional form, are the things we think of, such as Coke, Kleenex, and Advil. These are big, robust brands that are recognizable in both in messaging and packaging. Messaging and packaging are the two key components in effective brand strategy. If your message and package are different, or fragmented and not uniform, you will confuse your audience.

When creating a brand for yourself, here are a few things you should consider:

Understanding the "look" of the market

Each market has its own look and feel. For some markets, it will be a consistency in color, messaging or packaging. For others, it may just be a "feeling." For example, if you're writing a basic book about anything, à la the *For Dummies* guides, these brands would be super-simple, clear, and often yellow. This is because yellow is associated with learning. While consumers may recognize your business brand, your book might need an entirely different look. Getting to know your market is the #1 thing you should do when you're thinking of developing your brand.

Identity crisis: who are you?

So who are you, really? This isn't meant to be a psychological exam. It is meant to be an in-depth look at your brand, your market, as well as your current focus and future goals. There's a saying that goes: "If you don't know what road you're on, any path will do." The same is true for your brand and your career. Define where you want to go, and then build to that message.

Brainstorm your brand

If necessary, get some outside help. Book branding doesn't have to be expensive, but it does have to be thorough. Understanding your brand and your message is important. If you don't control it, your consumer will. Additionally, since your book is an offshoot of your business, it'll be important to fold the two together seamlessly.

Delivering on a promise

Whatever you promise, you must deliver. In fact, promise less and deliver more. If you have promised the reader a guide to investing with penny stocks, don't just give them an overview of the stock market. If your message doesn't live up to its promise, you'll lose your reader, as well as a customer—probably forever.

The center of the universe—your website

As a business owner and new author, your website is the single most important piece of your brand. Yes, your book is important, but before readers get there, they will often find your website first. Here you'll need to decide if you're going to fold your book into your existing site, or create a new website for it. When I wrote *Red Hot Internet Publicity*, I simply added a page to my site that was found through the URL www.redhotinternetpublicity.com. The branding remained consistent, and I didn't have to build another site from scratch. Keep in mind that, while a separate website may make sense for some, it does require its own maintenance in the form of blogging and any optimization you may do to generate traffic.

Relevancy and Consistency

Trends are hard to predict. Though there are a lot of books out about trend prediction and what makes a trend "a trend," it's still tough to gauge when things will spark. Generally, I try to stay away from these types of predictions, mostly because now, more than ever. Trends can be affected by something as simple as an errant tweet or as big as a world crisis.

The key to creating a brand that is sustainable can be broken down into three key factors. First, develop an idea that locks into the needs of your market now. Secondly, understand how their opinions or needs might change over time. The last factor to consider is consistency. While you want to be flexible and offer what your consumer wants, you don't want to be so flexible that you're changing your model every quarter to support a changing market. Candidly, most markets don't change that fast. Even if you do experience a lot of change, your customers' core needs and values generally don't (and shouldn't) shift that rapidly.

I find that the perspective and input of friends, family, and other influencers can be a double-edged sword. While they can be helpful, these opinions could also create confusion in your brand.

Here's an example. A business client came to me with a project. He had a book he wanted to do that tied in nicely to his business. He was super clear on where he wanted it to go and what his brand would look like. Then he began soliciting views from people who weren't in his industry and weren't particularly his target market. The feedback he got, while intended to be helpful, ultimately distracted him from his goals. Could his book be adapted for schools? Possibly, but not likely. Could it become a resource for newlyweds? Again, a possible demographic, but not the majority.

When you're putting together the topic, direction, and brand for your book (and possibly your business), be sure to work with someone who you have no ties to beyond a business arrangement. This person can help you be objective and ferret out ideas and targets that may not be your primary markets. Chasing a million ideas isn't helpful. Define the market, the relevancy, and then stick with your message.

In terms of consistency, to some degree, this harks back to getting advice from a bunch of people, but it's also about how we market ourselves in general. Find your core message and stick with it. Changing your message and focus too frequently will confuse your consumer which ultimately won't help you sell books. This also helps to drive the book process forward, too. Whether you're writing it yourself or hiring someone to do it, you need to understand the heart of your message.

Loving the Spin-Offs

We love the spin-off, don't we? For years, they were one of the biggest money drivers in television. But it doesn't have to be limited to TV shows; it works well for books, too. When you're creating your book, think about what other things you can create to help generate revenue, like audio clips, workbooks, mini-books, video programs, behind-the-scenes, and webinars. All of these things can help bring in additional revenue. Your one idea or one book could lead to hundreds of other spin-offs.

Hiring Someone Else to Write Your Book

If writing your own book seems too daunting, you might want to consider hiring a ghostwriter to help you finish the job. I've had a book done by a ghost (I'll let you guess which one. Hint: it's not this one). If you find the right ghostwriter, it can be a great process and a fantastic investment. Most of the busier authors, speakers, and business owners not only have a ghost writing their book, but also their tweets, Facebook updates, and blog posts.

I sat down with Michael Levin, who has helped author numerous best-sellers, and talked with him about what it takes to find a good ghostwriter, and what you should look for. Here is what he had to say:

~ Michael Levin Interview with Penny Sansevieri ~

Question 1: How can someone find a good ghostwriter?

You can find a ton of writers online, so before you start Googling writers, ask around. Word of mouth is usually the best way to find a really good ghostwriter. There may be someone in your network who has written a book with a ghost, so you want to start there. You've got to be very careful, because there are no licensing standards or boards for ghostwriters—anyone can put out a shingle and say, "I write books." So the question becomes, how can you know who you can trust?

The first thing to identify is whether ghostwriting books is the primary function of the writer, or whether writing books is just one of many services the writer offers, and most likely not the primary service. Most freelance writers cast a broad net, and they will claim to write anything under the sun, from business cards and brochures to websites to social media to multi-volume series. I've seen people make the mistake of saying, "This person says he does ghostwriting! I could probably get the book done and save a lot of money!"

Typically, however, people who write short-form materials have limited or no experience writing books, and you certainly don't want them going to school on your nickel. So that's why the first consideration is whether the ghost actually specializes in books, or whether book writing is one claim, perhaps unsubstantiated, among many in the writer's marketing materials.

Let's say you've got someone in mind whose website indicates that ghostwriting is a specialty, or, ideally, their main function. Great. Check out multiple samples of the ghostwriter's work, so you can determine whether they sound different one from each other, or if they all sound the same. If the ghostwriter you're considering is not willing or able to share sample chapters, consider this to be a major red flag.

Next, you want to be able to talk with past clients. If the ghostwriter doesn't readily provide you contact information for at least three past clients, consider this to be another red flag.

You may also want to "test drive" the writer to make sure that he or she is right for you. Ask if the ghostwriter you're interested in is willing to work on a test drive basis. A great ghostwriter will understand that you just want to make sure that there's a good fit. Planning a good book is even harder than writing a good book. If your person's capable of creating a really good plan, based on just a couple of hours of meeting with you, then you know you have the right person.

In ghostwriting, as in everything else, you get what you pay for. The problem is that most people who are contemplating hiring a ghostwriter have never written a book before. I was quoted in *Bloomberg Business Week* as saying that, "For $5,000, you can get a ghostwriter to write a book for you, and then paint your house." But how good will the book be?

There are two factors here. First is that many writers, even many good writers, are allergic to business, and don't know how to price themselves fairly. The problem is that for every diamond in the rough, low-fee-charging, low-self-esteem writer out there, there are dozens more who charge a very small amount of money because they deliver, quite frankly, very low level of quality. The most expensive way to buy ghostwriting is to try to get it on the cheap and then turn around and have to start all over again with someone else. I'm not even sure the phrase, "You get what you pay for," applies to low-cost ghostwriting. You're still paying $5,000 or $10,000, but you're getting nothing.

Question 2: What makes a good ghostwriter?

Great question. Great ghostwriters absorb and organize substantial amounts of material quickly. They're able to see patterns others might not be able to see. They're able to stand in the shoes of the reader and ask the questions for which the reader would want answers. They're able to write in the voice of the client, no matter how different the client's voice is from their own. They're able to interview well. They can take criticism—meaning they don't have a diva or artiste mentality. They recognize that they're performing a job for a client who needs to be satisfied, and that the client's satisfaction is the primary measure of success—not their own feelings about how the book ought to be.

In that sense, great ghostwriters are flexible. They can hear and understand the perspective of the client. They know when to fight for a different approach, and they also know when to give in. They can see the big picture and the small details.

Question 3: Talk to me about contracts. What should an author expect when signing on with a ghost?

The way I like to think of agreements is that they simply specify what the responsibilities are for each of the parties involved. The writer's job is to organize, interview, write, rewrite, and if that's part of the deal, publish the book. The client's role is to be available for interviews, respond quickly with comments and changes, and, of course, pay on time! So what you're looking for in an agreement with a ghostwriter is, above all, clarity. What are the deadlines? What are the deliverables? Are you getting the manuscript chapter by chapter, in chunks, or all at once?

There has to be a solid, legal agreement between the parties. The reality is that, in ghostwriting, a great deal can go wrong. You have to have what lawyers call a "meeting of the minds" on every issue—is the writer's name going to appear on the book? Is the client obligated to acknowledge the writer somewhere in the book? What if payments are late? What if a dispute arises? What about refunds?

Question 4: How do ghostwriters work, generally?

I learned that my clients were way too busy to devote much more than a couple of hours a week to their ghostwriting project. So at BusinessGhost we evolved an approach in which we avoid long, drawn-out interviews over a broad range of topics, and instead we simply ask the client for an hour per chapter per week. We basically ask the client to do a file dump on us of everything he or she has ever known, thought, experienced, believed, witnessed, or imagined about the topic of that chapter. Is this the way ghostwriting works generally? I don't think so. But maybe it should!

~ Thanks to Michael Levin for supplying these answers. ~
You can find Michael at BusinessGhost.com

Several years ago, I attended my first ghostwriting conference. It was clear from this event that ghostwriting is a profession that will keep growing. As you get busier, a talented ghostwriter can be a fantastic person to have on the team. The conference was an amazing collection full of writers who have been creating books "in the shadows" for many years. What I found was that their talent isn't just limited to books. Some do blog postings, white papers, and even Twitter updates. Finding a good ghostwriter can really help you speed up the process of book completion, and take a lot of the burden of creating it off your shoulders.

Writing Right:
The Importance of Editing

"No passion in the world is equal to the passion to alter someone else's draft."
– William Shakespeare

Sometimes the difference between a mildly successful book and a wildly successful book is one thing: editing. The importance of a well-edited book cannot be overstated, and if this is one area where you're hoping to skimp, think again.

Look at it this way: Your book is your résumé. You'd never consider sending out a résumé full of typos, would you? So, like a résumé, your book should be letter-perfect.

You'll be surprised by how helpful a good editor can be, says Faith Freewoman, owner of Demon for Details Manuscript Editing www.demonfordetails.com/). Content editors especially are not only interested in what you're saying, how you're saying it, and whether it's accurate. They are often familiar with the subject of your book, and could come up with questions and suggestions that hadn't occurred to you (in spite of the wonderfully detailed analysis you'll do by following the suggestions of this book).

There are basically three levels of editing: content editing, copy/line editing, and proofreading. Most smart authors, and especially authors who plan to self-publish, use all three. And there are editors who do both content and copy/line editing, and editing organizations which provide all three services.

Friends, Family, & Aunt Tilly

And don't make the mistake of depending on family and friends to do your editing. There are two reasons why you shouldn't:

First, they will probably tell you what they think you want to hear, because they love you, because you're friends, and/or because they think it's what you want.

Second, even if your Aunt Tilly teaches college English, she's most likely not trained to notice the kind of nit-picky details a great editor would pick up on.

Lastly, because Aunt Tilly knows you, she's used to your "voice," the way you normally express yourself, which might or might not be appropriate for your book.

Content Editors

Content editors look at the big picture. Has the content has kept the promise of the title? They'll also keep the book's structure, organization, consistency in mind. Most importantly, they should be ensuring that the "voice"—which refers to the way you express yourself, is both commanding and credible. Content editors address your use of language as much as the facts, figures, and ideas presented. They're alert for flow, word choices, character quirks, and more, that can be tweaked to make your book even better, highlighting your voice and your style. They'll often suggest alternatives or give examples. These services can be especially helpful if you are also interested in doing speaking engagements.

Copy/Line Editors

Copy/line editors are also concerned with use of language, but are more focused on grammar (i.e. sentence structure, punctuation, word choice), spelling, word usage (i.e. homophones, words that sound like the correct word, but are spelled differently, and mean something entirely different, like vice and vise), repetitiveness, clarity and conciseness. Like a good content editor, a good copy editor will note places where they think—based on your writing style and author voice—the writing can be improved.

Proofreaders

A proofreader is normally hired to do the final read-through of your book, watching for errors. After a certain number of times, even a top-notch editor can read past things like omitted words or missing punctuation.

Get a Sample Edit

In all three cases, it's best to narrow down your choices to two or three, and request a sample edit from each of the levels of editor you plan to use. Most editors and proofreaders will provide a sample of 5-10 double spaced pages for free, or for a nominal fee. The sample edits will show you, for example, if a particular content or copy/line editor is going to basically rewrite your book—which in most cases you don't want. That approach can indicate a lack of respect for you as an author. And if later you want a longer sample, simply ask. Most editors will be happy to work it out.

What you want are editors who notice things you didn't, who are positive but clear about things that need fixing, and whose suggestions not only sound like you said it, but make you feel better about your content and presentation. Once you compare the samples, it's usually pretty easy to choose the editor who's right for you.

What to Ask Potential Editors Before You Request a Sample Edit

Before you send off the sample of your book to a prospective editor, here are some things you'll want to ask them:

1. **Have you edited many books?** Editing books requires different skills than editing speeches, articles, blogs and presentations. It certainly requires more stamina, as well as the ability to keep the details and structure as a complete work in mind while editing word for word.

2. **What types of books have you edited?** Some editors are comfortable working in both fiction and nonfiction, but it can help if the editor is familiar with your subject, even if he or she has had to get help making DIY repairs and your book is a self-help guide. If your prospective editor doesn't feel able to edit your subject, you can always ask for referrals.

3. **What are your typical editing rates for a book of this type and size?** Most editors have their rates and services clearly stated on their web site, so it's good to read those first and then ask questions.

4. **What is your average turnaround time?** An editor is also a businessperson, and you have the right to expect a production schedule, and to commit to some deadlines of your own so your editor can stay on target. It can get complicated if you're using two or three editors, because, unless they already work together, or they're willing to coordinate with each other, you'll be responsible for coordinating their schedules.

What Should I Expect from My Editor?

Here are some tips for finding that eagle-eyed editor:

An editor:

- Will tell you up front whether or not they feel qualified and able to handle your project, and will either refer you to more qualified editors, or suggest what you should look for.

- Delivers professional, courteous service, and replies to to project questions within 24 hours for both emails and phone messages, weekends not included).

- Provides a clear, understandable letter of agreement or work-for-hire contract. The agreement should detail out how the professional relationship will work, including scope, fees, payment, deadlines, confidentiality assurances, and so on.

- Uses Microsoft Word's "Track Changes" and "Comments" features to detail recommended corrections, to make suggestions, or to ask clarifying questions.

- When the edits are complete, provides you with a file which includes all corrections, suggestions, and comments. Most can easily provide a file with all edits accepted and comments, suggestions and questions still available.

- Works through your manuscript at least twice if you have agreed to have both content AND copy editing done. Usually you get the manuscript back after the first pass, so you can respond to the editor's changes, questions, comments and uggestions before they do the final edit.

- Provides honest and courteous feedback.

- Is dependable in terms of establishing and meeting deadlines.

- Is honest.

- Maintains your confidentiality.

- Encourages you to remember that you have the final say about any and all suggestions, corrections or changes.

The best editors know they are an author's support staff, not the author! What happens if your editor recommends that you eliminate a chapter, or use a completely different approach, and you disagree? A good editor will come up with some new approaches, and/or defer to your judgement if you feel your original version is best.

Pay close attention to the sample edit. If the editor has attempted to rewrite your writing, it's a bigger red flag than if they don't change enough. Also, you probably shouldn't choose an editor who promises to get you a publishing contract.

What's it Going to Cost?

Rates for editing do vary, but generally you can expect to pay anywhere from 1 to 3 cents per word or $50-100 an hour for editing. Again, get this rate in writing along with the quote. A good editor should be able to tell you up front what it will cost and submit a firm estimate to you.

Don't forget to ask about their payment schedule. Some will charge 50% upfront and 50% upon completion; some will bill you every two weeks if you're being billed by the hour, or any number of variations. Find out what methods of payment they accept, when they invoice and how long you have to send in the payment (due upon receipt, net 15, net 30, for example).

How to Make the Most of Your Editing Experience

Now that you've hired an editor, how can you make the most of your collaboration? Here are a few tips for how to have a harmonious working relationship and get the most out of it, in terms of both a learning experience for you, and the final product:

- Stay in touch. Ask questions. Let your editor know if you are running behind (so they can reschedule). Share ideas and links. The best way to work with an editor is to establish a congenial working relationship, and communication is the key.

- If you have strong convictions about style, make it very clear, and in detail, even if you've chosen your editor or editors because their style suits you.

- Just as you expect accurate timelines from your editors, your editors also expect you to be on target with your deadlines. Many editors work on multiple projects at once. Be sure to let them know as soon as possible if you can't meet your deadline, so they can adjust their schedules and let you know how your change will affect the rest of the schedule.

- Expect to pay more if you submit a substantially revised chapter or an added chapter once your editor begins work. If you add work not covered in the original work agreement, your editor needs to be compensated.

- Remember you have the right to veto any change your editor recommends or suggests. It's YOUR book!

- BUT! If your editor comes back with some alternative solutions to what they feel needs work, give it consideration. Their job is to see both forest and trees, and if you listen to suggestions, they might even trigger your own solution.

- If you prefer to communicate by email and your editor prefers long phone conversations, you may not be a good match. And vice versa.

- Once you've handed your manuscript to your editor, respond quickly to questions so you don't add to the turnaround time.

~ Thanks to Faith Freewoman
of Demon for Details Manuscript Editing. ~

You can find her at www.demonfordetails.com, or by emailing freewoman-business@att.net.

Book Proposals Make the Best Books

Have you ever seen a book proposal or maybe done one? Book proposals are what publishers or agents use to help them decide if they want to publish a book. The reason I love book proposals is because they force you, the writer, to be very detailed, and analyze the book at a granular level. This process can help to expedite your book development, because you've essentially created the skeletal structure of the book. Now all you have to do is fill in the gaps. Ready to start your own book proposal? Here's a quick how-to: www.janefriedman.com/start-here-how-to-write-a-book-proposal/

Can You Judge a Book
by Its Cover?

"In America, only the successful writer is important; in France,
all writers are important; in England, no writer is important;
and in Australia, you have to explain what a writer is."
– Geoffrey Cottrell

You most certainly can judge a book by its cover. In fact, one of your most effective sales tools is your book's cover. Did you know that if someone sees your book on a physical or even virtual bookshelf, you have less than thirty seconds to sell it? People are attracted to books by stunning colors and catchy titles. Remember, book covers not only impact your book, but your marketing materials as well.

The main color of your cover will probably reveal a general theme or set the tone for your marketing package. Some business owners ask me if their branding should be part of their book's color scheme. I'd say no in most cases.

Your book's niche or subject matter should determine the look and feel of your book, not your business. You want to stay consistent with your market, and you want to look professional. A great piece of advice someone once gave me, was to peruse the merchandise in a bookstore. Spend an afternoon, or as much time you can, looking over books that are similar to yours. Decide what works and what does not. Then have a cover designed that will attract your audience. While most on-demand publishers will do this for you, you want to enter into that part of the process with a full understanding of what you want, and what your final product should look like. If it starts to get too complicated, consider hiring a graphic designer.

This is what the designer of this book shared with me:

First and foremost, your cover must suit your topic and speak to your audience. Consider color psychology when you develop the palette for your book. Color, when used properly, will set a tone, create a feeling, and provide a visual statement without you having to say a word.

Many people, especially women, experience a visceral response to color and color combinations. If you know your audience, you will know which colors will reach your market. Ultimately, what you want to do is to attract and hold your reader's attention.

Crimson red is considered an aggressive color; it is associated with blood, fire and passion. Used in large quantities, it can sometimes be overwhelming. However, if it is used as an accent color, it will draw the eye and command attention.

Yellow is the sunshine color, associated with optimism, happiness and radiance. It is the perfect highlight color since it is the first color your eye sees. It is also the color that will fatigue the eyes most quickly and should be used sparingly.

Sage green and lavender are healing colors, and have been used effectively in marketing throughout the ages—John Deere tractors are green; they chose green because it is often associated with safety.

There really is no wrong color choice, as long as you choose something appropriate to your topic.

When it comes to red, think of the film *Schindler's List*. The entire movie is in black and white except for the scene when the little girl runs across the screen wearing red. How powerful was that? Would you remember the scene if she had been wearing blue? Would it stand out in your memory if the movie was in color? Probably not.

Where business titles are concerned, consider a simple look. There's a book called *Rework* by Jason Fried and David Hansson. The cover is simple: a crumpled piece of paper on a black background, with the title and the author's name above and below the balled-up paper, on the same black background. Nothing says "rework" more than a discarded piece of paper.

The cover for *Likeable Social Media* by Dave Kerpen is similar in its simplicity. It has a thumbs-up on the cover, nothing more. It's a universal symbol for being liked online, and everyone recognizes it.

Another example of a successful book with a simple cover is *Good to Great*, which nearly every entrepreneur knows or has read. The book is red, so it pops off of the shelf. The word 'Great' is written in big, bold letters so it, too, pops off of the page.

Each market will have different looks. If you're writing in New Age, you might see a lot of sage and lavender, soft tones, and smooth lines. For self-help, the style will be different still. Get to know your market, and spend time getting to know what you like and don't like about the covers in your target market. Then turn it over to someone who knows how to design books. Why is this important? Much like what we covered when it came to editors and their strengths being in a certain genre, designing business cards, letterhead, and folders is very different from book cover design.

I've seen too many covers where a designer has tried to do too much. If you try cramming too much information on the cover, the message is almost inevitably lost in the process.

Let's say you've decided to hire a cover designer for your book cover. What are some of the things you should be looking for from this professional?

Well, number one is a portfolio, which you can usually find on the designer's website. If you're considering a designer whose work you love, then you're on the right track, but if you look at his or her portfolio and don't find anything you like, chances are the design for your book cover will be equally off-putting. Next, you want to look for someone who understands your market. Sometimes designers will have specialties; other times they might read your entire book (or most of it) to get a real sense of your audience.

In either case, your designer should spend a considerable amount of time getting to know you, your niche, and your reader. Try to find a designer with a style matching that of your prospective reader. If you're looking for innovative, new, and flashy, for example, you probably don't want to use a conservative designer.

Last but not least, choose a designer who is familiar with your industry and understands the importance of reaching your audience. Your designer is your partner, and you should feel completely comfortable with them. A great designer will listen to your needs and bring your vision to life. And, as with editing, there's no room for ego when it comes to cover design; this is your baby.

Some tips to help you create an outstanding cover for your book:

Front Cover

Contrast is important. Draw attention to your book by using a lighter background with darker-color type, or vice versa. Avoid choosing a color for your title that gets lost in the background.

Make sure the title and subtitle are in different fonts to draw a distinction between the two.

Don't use all uppercase letters; it can give a very angry impression. Instead, use both uppercase and lowercase letters.

As a rule of thumb, the title should be visible from about 12 feet away, which means using letters no smaller than 24 point (1/3 inch), and preferably 36 point (1/2 inch) or larger.

It's often tempting to mimic the big-name authors and put your name in big, bold type at the top of the book. I don't recommend it.

Publishers will do it for big-name authors because they are the brand, and their name will draw an audience all on its own.

You might say, "Well, I'm a brand, too!" And perhaps you are. You need to make that call for yourself, but consider the front cover your most valuable real estate. Where do you really want to put the emphasis?

Back Cover

The back cover should list the benefits of the book. Remember, moments after being engaged by your front cover, readers are going to flip your book over to read the back cover.

Here are nine essential elements for creating back cover copy according to copywriter Casey Demchak:

1. Start with a headline that makes or implies a promise

Headlines have two simple goals: engage the attention of readers and drive them into your body copy. You don't need zippy, clever, sexy headlines to do this.

In fact, simple headlines are usually the most enticing. Start your back cover headline with an action word and then state or imply a promise of what readers can expect to gain from your book. Here are a few examples.

Learn to Shift Smoothly into a Champion's Mindset
Discover How to Generate Unlimited Wealth
Find Out What Drives Serial Killers to Act

Thought-provoking questions are also a great way to grab readers.

Did LBJ Know JFK Would Die in Texas?
Know the Secret to Attracting Success Like a Magnet?
Could You Escape from the Most Dangerous Place on Earth?

2. Make your copy "at-a-glance" friendly

If your headline draws readers in, don't lose them by using large blocks of text to fill out your back cover. Instead, make it "at-a-glance" friendly by employing a liberal use of headlines, subheads, short paragraphs and bullet points.

This common sales writing technique creates a lot of open space around your copy, which visually makes it look fast and easy to read.

3. Choose exactly the right voice

Create a definite, confident voice for your back cover. Depending on your topic, your writing should emanate authority, compassion, wisdom, insight, humor, suspense, intrigue, mystery, etc. Choose a voice for your back cover that matches your book. Then, fuel it with emotion.

4. Create a powerful rhythm

Think of the movie trailers you've seen for the films you love. They move at a steady rhythm and pace. This is because their creators know they only have one minute to convince you to watch a two-hour movie.

The same can be said for a back cover. You've got one page to motivate people to read your entire book. After you've written your back cover, it should have a beat and pulse to it that you can snap your fingers to as you read it.

5. Focus on what your book is about—not on what happens

It's certainly acceptable to write about what happens in your book. However, focus your back cover much more on how readers will benefit from your book. What curiosity will you satisfy? What challenge will you help readers overcome? What itch are you going to scratch?

6. Stir up human emotions

The only marketing messages that really move us are ones that grip us on an emotional level. Always describe the benefits readers will derive from your book in emotional human-value terms.

Think of it this way: you don't read about anti-aging skin creams so you can get rid of wrinkles. You read about anti-aging skin creams to get rid of wrinkles, so you'll feel more youthful and vibrant.

You don't read a murder mystery to find out who did it. You read a murder mystery to stimulate your imagination and create a sense of intrigue and excitement within yourself.

No matter what your book is about, your crowd will read it to fuel specific emotions within them. Identify what those emotions are and use your back cover copy to stir them up.

7. Leave them wanting more

This technique requires a little practice. Always conclude your back cover in a manner that leaves your readers begging for more. Give them the sizzle, but not the steak. Always conclude your back cover so readers have no choice but to flip through your table of contents as they're reaching for their wallet.

8. Endorsements

If you've collected reviews or endorsements from public figures, trade papers, well-known industry professionals, or respected literary publications—make room for at least one or two of them on your back cover!

9. Add your bio

Although it isn't an absolute necessity, most authors include a two- or three-line bio in the lower portion of their back cover.

Find out more about Casey Demchak and his services at
www.caseydemchak.com.

Spine

Make sure your name and the title of the book are prominent and easy to read.

Don't use a complicated font. Keep it simple.

Did You Know?

If you think the front cover gets an unfair 30-second judgment call, the back cover only gets 15 seconds.

It's What's Inside that Counts

If you think the work stops at your cover design, think again. The interior design of a book can also make or break a sale, and the more you know about this somewhat involved process, the better equipped you'll be to make the right decisions when it comes to interior choices.

Often, your cover designer can also assist you with your interior book design. When that's the case, you'll have someone on board who already knows your book. If your cover designer can't accommodate your interior needs, then you'll have to do some more shopping.

Much like your cover designer, one of the most important things will be to find a designer who knows your topic, understands your niche, and can create something appealing to your reader. Your designer should be willing to become intimate with your book so they can understand exactly what it will take to bring it to life. The overall design, layout, typeface choice, and use of illustrations, graphics, or photography should complement the book visually.

If your book is professional, you would be well served to stay with classic fonts like Times. Be sure to employ lots of white space for a serious book, because to clutter your pages is to muddle your message. A great way to break up a serious how-to topic is to employ breakout boxes that offer little tidbits of information and interesting facts that would otherwise look odd within the body of your text.

Lastly, study your competition and see how book covers and designs in your subject area are reaching your market—presentation will often sell your book before your reader even reads the first sentence. A well-thought-out book will engage your reader with a classy package that suits your niche perfectly and shows professionalism.

You want your book to look as professional as possible, and you want it to set you apart from the competition. The idea is to entice the reader to examine your book more closely, and then buy, while you avoid looking like an amateur. Lack of attention to detail in design can mean a potential reader will pass by your book and pick up the the more professional-looking one next to it.

Have you ever picked up a book because you "liked the look of it"? This is exactly what I'm talking about. The look, the feel, the entire package. Remember, when it comes to book promotion, everything counts, and it's not *Field of Dreams*. Just because you wrote it doesn't mean people will beat a path to your door. You have to make sure it's packaged correctly. You don't have to be the world's best designer to appreciate a good-looking product. A better design will also show your reader how serious you are about your work.

Here are some guidelines about interior design:

Layout

Just like cover design, interior pages should not be cluttered. Trying to squeeze too many elements or too much text on a page is a turnoff. A reader can be overwhelmed, not knowing where to look first, so keep the pages simple.

A reasonably-sized gutter (margin) between the edge of the page and where the text lies is at least 1/2 inch on the outside edge, top, and bottom, and 3/4 of an inch on the inside gutter, especially if the page count of your book is more than 128 pages. This extra space on the inside allows for the bend in the page as you open the book, and makes it a little easier to read without having to hold the book at an awkward angle. It also avoids forcing the pages so far apart that the binding splits. Most printers give certain specifications for page setup that pertain to their presses, so it's always a good idea to check with your printer first, and give your designer the relevant specifications for their design.

Body Copy and Other Text

Body copy should be left justified. Breakout boxes or bulleted items should appear ragged right, also known as flush left, and be contained in a smaller-width box. If they are not contained in boxes and appear in between paragraphs of text, use a larger indent to show the reader that this is a block of extra information that's not to be missed. Using a bullet point at the start of each sentence in a breakout box is also a good way to catch the reader's eye.

Folios (Headers and Footers)

Most pages have a folio (header or footer) either at the top or bottom of the page. A folio is what contains the title of the book, sometimes the author's name, as well as the chapter title and page number. Some books put page numbers at the foot of the page, with the book title at the top; others carry the book title at the top of the left page and the chapter title at the top of the right page. Page numbers most commonly appear on the outside edge of a page or the center. Remember to keep a fair distance of white space between your body copy and your folios. Again, you don't want your text to look cluttered or cramped. Anywhere from a ¼ inch to a ½ inch is a good guide.

Typefaces and Fonts

Once again, think about the nature of your book. If it is nonfiction, with hard facts and a serious tone, avoid fancy typefaces. Anything remotely "curly" will soften the look of your book, sending the message to your reader that your book could be somewhat light-hearted. For nonfiction, opt for a more sophisticated or traditional typeface instead.

Times New Roman is one of the most common fonts, and is installed on most computers, but many designers advise authors to use something other than Times New Roman, so it looks like you put more thought into it. Some others to choose from include Crown, Century, New Baskerville, Galliard, Garamond, Tribune or Stone.

Don't be limited by what is available on your computer's font list. There are thousands of free fonts on the Internet for you to choose from. Just do a search for "free downloadable fonts" in any search engine, and you will be amazed at what comes up as a result. If you are looking for something more exclusive, and don't mind paying for a well-designed typeface, check out websites such as fontbureau.typenetwork.com, emigre.com or fonts.com.

Serif versus Sans Serif

When a designer talks about a serif typeface, they mean fonts like Times New Roman or Century Schoolbook, where the characters (letters) have accents or curves. The French word serif defines those accents at the end of the main strokes of a character. For example, look at a capital T in the Times font. The small downward curves that appear at each end of the cross on the top and the inverted curves at the foot of the letter are known as serifs.

Sans is the French word meaning "without." Now look at a capital T in Helvetica or Arial. The character doesn't have those little accents, thus making them sans serif typefaces. Sans serif fonts are used mostly for breakout boxes, one- or two-word bulleted items, lists, headlines, and credits for illustrations and pictures. Attractive sans serif typefaces to consider include Franklin Gothic, News Gothic, Universe, Futura, Gill Sans and Stone Sans.

Type Size

Another important part of clear, legible interior design is the size of type you use to present your words. Consider your market. A reading book for young children or the elderly usually requires a larger-print format. Choose a size from 14 to 18 point The words should be presented clearly on the page and kept at a minimum. An adult fiction novel, however, may run at 9 to 11 point, with about 32 to 35 lines of text on each page, depending on the book size. Leading—the spacing between each line—must also be considered; it must not be too tight or too airy. Look for balance, with spacing that reflects all the other elements of design previously mentioned. If lines are spaced too closely together, or too far apart, readers can very easily lose their places, either by reading the same line twice, or missing out on chunks of text. This can become frustrating, and if that happens, a reader will ultimately put the book down because of the distraction, without even realizing why.

Chapter Headings

You don't have to use the same typeface for your chapter headings that you have used for your body copy. In fact, it helps if you don't. You avoid making your book look the same all the way through, and therefore boring.

This is where you get to be a bit more creative. It's a way to indicate to the reader that they have reached a new stage of the book. It's a no-brainer, of course, but also a chance to present your book in a different way to everyone else. Pick a font that complements your body copy (serif or sans serif), that also has that little something special to make it appear attractive and inviting.

Some authors use a symbol, such as a star or flower, with a decorative typeface that continues throughout the book. This helps brand the book, and pulls all the different sections together. Fonts such as Zapf Dingbats, Webdings, and Wingdings are standard symbol fonts that you can browse through to find an icon suitable for your book, or you can have a designer create a symbol for you. Decorative borders are another way to express some individuality, but remember, don't overdo it.

If in doubt, think "less is more." Keep designs simple, elegant, and sophisticated, and not too trendy (unless your book calls for it). A good design is meant to enhance the message of a book for the readers, not to distract them from it.

Cover Images

If you're thinking of getting a cover photo for your book, you can browse through a number of online stock photo shops. When deciding on a cover photo for *The Cliffhanger*, I waded through 2,500 photos before I found exactly the right one. That's how significant this process is. Photos should typically be about 300 dpi (dots per inch) for cover images. This is what most on-demand publishers will accept, but check with them first, since their requirements may differ.

When using a cover image, I recommend going through a stock-photo company unless you have a picture you want to use and the necessary permissions to put it on the cover of your book. Don't shortchange yourself on this. Assume that your book is going to be a national best-seller. You don't want to take any chances with copyright infringements here. People will see the picture and often recognize it, so get your permission in writing.

A few stock-photo companies I've used are:

www.gettyimages.com
www.photospin.com
www.istockphoto.com
stock.adobe.com

Back Cover Worksheet

"Politics is not a bad profession. If you succeed there are many rewards, if you disgrace yourself you can always write a book."
– Ronald Reagan

Category: _____

Headline: _____

What is your book about? _____

_____

_____

_____

_____

_____

Benefits: _____

You will learn/discover: _____

_____

_____

_____

_____

Why are you qualified to write this book?_____

_____

_____

_____

_____

_____

_____

_____

_____

_____

Section Three

Getting Ready to Go to Market

"I write for the same reason I breathe; because if I didn't, I would die."

– Isaac Asimov

Why You Need to "Get Ready" Before You Go to Market

"The sale begins when the customer says yes."
– Harvey MacKay

Before you leave the house to run errands, you make a list of groceries to buy, and anything else you want to accomplish. The same holds true before you start marketing your book. You'll need to have a plan in place before you begin.

If your marketing plan is to put your book up on Amazon and hope it turns into a best-seller, then let me be the first to give you the bad news: you might sell one copy.

However, if you're a successful businessperson, you already know that nothing comes from nothing. Success is the result of hard work and a solid plan. This section is all about helping you build a solid marketing plan for your book.

We will touch on how to find your book's selling point(s), what makes your book unique, and how to do a solid market analysis. Additionally, we're going to teach you how to set yourself up for success on Amazon, and the ever-important top of the pyramid: how to name and price your book for success.

Are there other paths to success? Sure there are. But as the adage goes, work smarter, not harder. At Author Marketing Experts, we are always striving to improve our processes, and in our ever-changing world, there are always great new things we can do to improve the success of our efforts. But, with that said, we'd love to help you avoid reinventing the wheel by showing you our time-tested marketing process, and help get your new business card—your book—started out right!

What's Your Book's USP?

Your USP, or unique selling proposition, is important. You need to know why your book is different, why it matters, and, moreover, why it will matter to your reader. Use the following exercise to help determine your USP.

Who have you written this book for?

_____

_____

_____

_____

_____

_____

_____

_____

_____

What problem does your book solve for this core target audience? What need does it meet or desire does it fulfill?

_____

_____

_____

_____

_____

_____

_____

_____

_____

_____

_____

Provide more details about the problem, need, or desire your book addresses, and discuss an example.

_____

_____

_____

_____

_____

_____

_____

_____

_____

_____

_____

_____

Tell what your book does to address the problem, need, or desire, and how it achieves it in a unique way.

_____

_____

_____

_____

_____

_____

_____

_____

_____

_____

Finally, put it all together. What's unique about your book? What's your USP?

_____

_____

_____

_____

_____

_____

_____

_____

_____

_____

_____

_____

_____

Worksheet courtesy of Wheatmark, Inc.

Media Leads Ignite the Idea Wheel

If you're stuck for ideas, whether it's what to blog about, or additional topics to include in your book, try subscribing to a reporter requests and media leads service like HARO (helpareporterout.com). You'll be sent a daily (often several times a day) list of media leads, many in your area of expertise. The lists should spark plenty of ideas or blog topics, as well as new topics to add to your current book if it's still in production, or to start building the next book.

Book Marketing Analysis: What are Your Strengths and Weaknesses?

"If you wait until you're really sure, you'll never take off your training wheels."
– Cynthia Copeland Lewis

Analyzing your own book can be tough, but it's often the first step in making sure you have a viable title. For this exercise, I'd like you to make an honest appraisal of your book's marketing strengths and weaknesses.

In order to get you started, I've given you a sample. See how many of these slots you can fill in on your own. The idea here is to create as many plusses and minuses as possible, because the more you know about your strong and weak points, the better you can address them both.

For example, in the first sample on the worksheet I recommend you look at other, more recognizable names, i.e. the authorities in your market. What might you do to be mindful of these weaknesses? Perhaps you could turn them into strengths by asking the industry authorities to endorse your book or write a foreword.

As you carefully consider your book's strengths and weaknesses, you'll start to see some marketing ideas take shape. We've started you off with examples in the first line.

My book's marketing strengths	My book's marketing weakness
It's the most current version out there on the topic.	There are a lot of big and recognizable names out there who could have written this. I am still building my platform.

Knowing Your Competition (and Why It Will Help You Sell More Books)

"I'd like to have money. And I'd like to be a good writer.
These two can come together, and I hope they will,
but if that's too adorable, I'd rather have money."
– Dorothy Parker

It's important to know your competition. We have discussed this several times in this book, but now it's time to get serious about it.

Carve out an hour to spend in a bookstore and make a list of all of the current competing titles. You should also do the same thing on Amazon, where you'll likely find even more titles.

There's an added reason to get to know your competition—so you can network with them, perhaps share advertising or marketing campaigns, or contribute articles to each other's newsletters. Frankly, you should! Why? Because most people don't buy just one copy of a particular niche. If someone buys mysteries, they generally buy across the same category. And mystery readers love mysteries, right? If someone buys a diet book or a self-help book, the same is true. And it's the reason stores cluster with other stores offering similar merchandise ... a bed and bath store, a mattress store, a fouton store, a furnishing store, and more, will occupy the same small mall area with remarkable results.

The idea is that you can compete more effectively if you know who your competition is, and team up with the other authors. So get to know the competition also publishing in your market, and learn what you can from the books that are already on the shelf.

Here's a quick checklist for you to take with you the next time you go into a bookstore. I recommend doing this for at least 5 to 10 of the top books in your category:

Author: _____

Author Website: _____

Book Title: _____

Year Published: _____

Publisher: _____

Retail Price: _____

What I like about this book: _____

_____

_____

_____

_____

_____

_____

What I'd change about this book: _____

_____

_____

_____

_____

_____

"You've already heard it a million times ... know your audience. As I wrote *Beyond the Blues: Treating Depression One Day at a Time,* I wrote each day of this daily meditation book with the vision of a person who is in desperate need of some encouragement, comfort, and support. I approach marketing and promotion with the same vision ... the vision of getting this book in the hands of some lost soul who may be in desperate need of some experience, strength, and hope."

– Edward F. Haas

Getting More Media Attention for Your Book and Business!

Getting media attention for your business, product, or book can be very effective way to launch a new product, or get some attention for your work. The problem is that in the age of the 24/7 news cycle, getting media attention is trickier now more than ever. The silver lining is that it's not impossible.

Feeding the Beast

The media is always looking for stories. Whether it's your story or someone else's, they need to feed their ravenous news cycle. You've no doubt noticed during a breaking news story that experts seem to crawl out of the woodwork. While you might not agree with some of the experts the media calls on, they all have one thing in common: they were media-ready. I'm not talking about being media trained (though that's important too). I'm talking about being really ready. They know their stuff, know their market, have developed good talking points, and in general are very solid experts.

Be What the Media Is Looking for

We work with a lot of authors who want major national media coverage. The problem is, few of them are truly ready for this calling.

As a marketing and PR expert, my focus is on getting the best media and marketing attention I can for our authors. At the same time, I'm an expert myself. I have authored 16 books, I blog weekly about marketing and, when warranted, I blog on breaking news in the industry. I can cite you chapter and verse of any recent statistics. I research trends and I know other experts who have done similar research that I can call upon. The point is, I know my market, and if you're going after national media attention, you had better know yours.

You, the Expert

Often I'll encounter an author or business owner who pretty much just wants me to make them famous. This isn't really possible. I mean, I guess it is if you want to run naked through Times Square (spoiler alert: it's already been done). Generally speaking, though, you need to do the work for the fame you seek.

Regardless of who you hire, you need to be the expert. This means that you're blogging consistently, your social media feed shows ideas you share with your followers, and you are focused on your industry. This means you know trends and stats, and other experts you can call on if needed. You've done your research, and, because you have, it will be clear to the media that you are an expert that they can call on. If someone who popped out of the box yesterday and wants national fame is not someone I'll work with. That said, by the same token, I'd certainly work with them to pitch them to their own regional market. Generally an untapped market, pitching to your own regional market can be hugely beneficial in expanding their platform, which is also the first step to building a national presence.

Know Your Media Markets

National media is not all created equal. It's important to know where your city ranks in the top 100 media markets. For example, if you're looking to pitch yourself to regional media in New York, this can be difficult, since the majority of that media is all national—in other words, they only cover news with national impact and implications. Some media professionals will even tell you that there's no such thing as regional media in New York, but I disagree. If you actually live and/or do business in that big city, consider pitching yourself to the five boroughs, and other outlying markets that are still hungry for news.

The main reason it's good to know where your market sits is because the closer you are to that number-one spot (out of 100), the harder it will be to get regional media for your message, and the more you might want to consider outlying areas. For example, Los Angeles, CA is the number 2 media market, and while LA has a lot of great regional papers, it's still a tough slog to capture their attention. There are, however, lots of great regional newspapers just a stone's throw from the heart of Los Angeles. Consider Orange County, Long Beach, Artesia, Santa Monica, and other nearby cities that often have their own local newspapers. Inclue dailies like the Orange County Register and the San Diego Union Tribune (San Diego is not too far to go for customers, and especially potential readers).

Here's a great link to all 100 media markets across the country, in case you want to see where your area fits in!
www.newsgeneration.com/broadcast-resources/
top-100-radio-markets/

Understanding Different Types of Media

It's crucial for you to understand that not all media are created equal. As I mentioned in the previous section, sometimes national media markets can also determine the trajectory of your campaign. That said, there are three tiers to media:

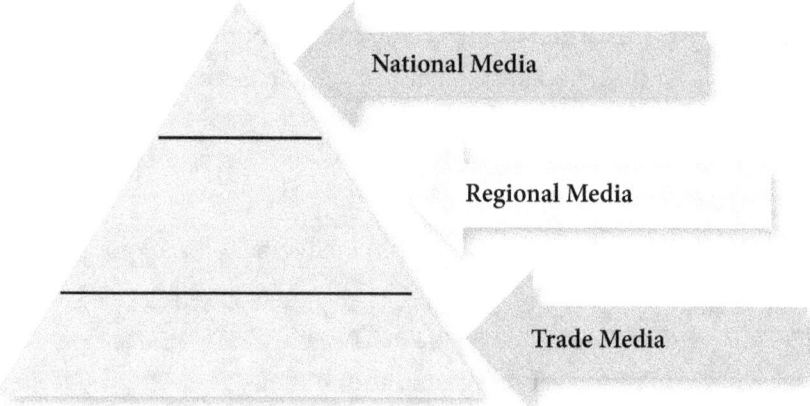

National Media

Regional Media

Trade Media

National media is what we are all familiar with and, of course, the smallest and busiest slice of this media pie. This includes big morning shows like CBS This Morning, Today on NBC, and Good Morning America. It also includes any major daytime talk show or evening newscast as well as national magazines and national newspapers such as *The Wall Street Journal, New York Times, Los Angeles Times,* and *The Washington Post.* All of these newspapers sit in big media markets, so by default they fall into the national media category.

The next rung on the ladder is **regional media**. This includes any media exclusive to a region, town, or city, and it's often some of the best and easiest media to grab. If you're promoting any local event that's open to the public, like a book signing or something along those lines, definitely pitch it to local media. Additionally, if you can offer a local spin to a story that's making national news, your regional media wants to hear from you.

The final rung, and potentially the largest, is **trade media**. This is any kind of media specific to a trade, hobby, or profession, such as golfer magazines, wrestling magazines, and writing publications. Podcasts and blogs dedicated to a focused profession or hobby could also be considered trade media. Some trade media can also exist very far off the grid in the form of newsletters specific to genealogy markets, or parenting newsletters, things like that. These can be a real gold mine if you can pitch them. They're much easier to gain access to if you're already an expert in that market. But remember, for any of these areas, you still need a solid, strong pitch.

The Art of the Perfect Pitch

Let's take a look at the best ways to craft and hone your pitch.

The Spin/Pitch

How you pitch is almost as important as what you pitch, and when it comes to pitching media, less is truly more. Imagine if you were working the CBS Evening News, and you have to ferret through 1,000 pitches a week. Surprisingly, this number is not an exaggeration, and often these numbers can be considerably higher. How would you manage to sift through that much email and still run a show? Well, you'd probably start by looking at the subject lines.

Your subject lines are often more important than your pitch. If your email subject line doesn't get people to open your email, then what's the point of the pitch, right? Keep it short and snappy and, most of all, relevant.

Back Up Your Statements

Now that the email is open, the statements you make need something weighty to support them. How do you do this? Cite studies if you have access to them, or cite other stories about this subject (if your story is a follow-up piece). In order to lend credibility to what you are saying or offering as a topic idea, you'll need to substantiate it with some facts. Make sure that if you quote statistics, that you provide a way for them to verify. Need to know where to find some statistics? Take a look at trade publications you subscribe to. Gallup polls are another great resource. You are the expert, so you should have basic backup at your fingertips.

Think HUH: Hip, Unique, and Helpful

Always, always be helpful with your pitches, because it's what the media will be looking for. How will this help my audience? Keep in mind that help can also be inspiring, educating, entertaining. It doesn't always have to be "help" in the general sense.

Keep It Short

If you can't share your idea in a paragraph, then keep reworking it till you can. There's an old media term called "above the fold". It generally applies the belief that anything that's above the newspaper fold is important, which is also the first thing readers see when looking at a paper. Your email should be no different. Keep it short, and do not make the media person scroll. If they like the pitch, they'll no doubt ask for more information, and that's when you can load them up with everything else you've got to share.

Don't ever send attachments with your first pitch. With thousands of pitches, the media has to sort through every week, you don't want yours getting lost in a spam filter because of an attachment. If you include an image of your product, find a way to include it in the text of your email. Otherwise, just provide the purchase link.

Finally, remember that most of us (and this includes media) looks at emails on our phones, and often in preview form. In addition to your subject line, consider adding a teaser at the top, or an enhanced subject line, before you get to the "dear so and so" portion of your pitch. I've found this to be super helpful to media, especially if you want to use that one sentence to elaborate even further on your subject line.

How to Tie Your Pitch into What's Trending

The media is always anchored to what's going on right now or, what might be coming up for them, so whenever there's a news story you can comment on, a looming holiday, or some other kind of "thing" out there you can comment on, make sure you have a pitch that's tight, targeted, and ready to go.

Figuring out how to pitch, or what to pitch, or how to phrase it, isn't always easy, but there are a couple of good schools you can go to to learn, and they're called the evening news and the newsstand. Next time you watch your nightly news broadcast, pay attention to how they tease stories before they go to a commercial (this is called the "bridge") and watch how newscasts often start out by teasing stories coming up later on in the broadcast. These teasers will give you a good sense of how the media likes to get their pitches, and the more your pitch can align with these preferences, the faster you could make it into the national news.

Next, stop by your local newsstand and just take a look at the teasers on the front of magazines. All of them are short, sweet, and good at enticing you to open the covers and see more. As with national news, these examples are another great way to start getting a sense of how the "spin/pitch" works.

Trends, Hot News Stories, and Seasonal Stuff

To get you started, here's a sampling of some pitches we've done in the past.

Holiday: Valentine's Day
Hook: Do You Know You Could Meet Mr. Right in a Soup Kitchen?
The story behind the hook: Our volunteerism author commented on how singletons are meeting their significant others while volunteering. While her book did not focus on singles and volunteerism, she knew enough about this topic to comment on it. Once we did our research, we learned that singles volunteer organizations were springing up all across the country.

Holiday: Christmas
Hook: Give Your Kids the Gift of Laughter this Holiday Season!
T**The story behind the hook** We were working with an author who specialized in the importance of humor and children. He offered ways to give kids the gift of a lifetime: laughter.

Calendar hook: Fire Prevention Week
Hook: How to Get Organized Without Resorting to Arson
The story behind the hook Our author had a book about organization, but the title pulled right into Fire Prevention Week, so while promoting it around other dates that supported organization, we also pushed it during Fire Prevention Week!

Calendar hook: Holidays
Hook: When Airplanes and Relatives Don't Leave on Time

The story behind the hook This was a humor-based book about family dynamics around the holidays. The media loved this, and we got tons of radio, print and TV for this hook! We also had the good luck (or bad, depending on your perspective) of a massive snowstorm that shut down the east coast and grounded most flights right after Thanksgiving, so it was a great local tie-in.

These are some subject lines we've used very recently to pitch national media, with very relevant and timely tie-ins to current news.

- Will Technology Vaporize Your Job?
- Is Fake News Making You Sick?
- Is Post-Election Stress Disorder Killing Us?
- Is Your "Cold" More Than Just a Virus?

The takeaway is for you to remember you can't do this in a vacuum. You must be out there and blogging, tweeting, and sharing your good ideas and helpful suggestions on social media. Making yourself attractive to the media is sort of like applying for a job. Your resume is polished, you show up on time, and have your expertise ready to share. Getting media attention is no different. It's a job interview, and it's the job of getting in front of a national audience. Do it right, and you won't be able to keep up with the interview requests.

Best Pitching Practices

Pitching is, to say the least, a tricky walk for most of us. Even though I've done media pitching for twenty years, I still sometimes struggle through a pitch, or struggle to keep it short, or to come up with the best subject line. But aside from the pieces we've discussed in this section, it's also important to know pitch practices, and the best ways to get email pitches noticed. Here are a few:

Pitch the Right People

The final and perhaps most important piece of this is to pitch the right people. While I know this goes without saying, it's amazing how often I hear folks pitching the wrong media targets. Know this: in most cases the media isn't going to pass along your pitch to the right person (read: they won't do your work for you), so make sure you're approaching the right person to start with.

Never, ever, ever pitch the host unless the show is so small the host is also ferreting through pitches and running the show. A lot of times folks are keen on pitching hosts of shows, or the editor of a magazine, or whatever, but hosts and magazines editors generally aren't vetting pitches and, while they might pass your pitch along to someone who will, they will most likely simply delete it.

If you've pitched bloggers in the past and are now turning your attention to national media, know this: a national media pitch should be much more formal than a blogger pitch. For media, you need to prove your know your stuff right there in the pitch, whereas a blogger might take a bit of time to peruse your website and get to know you before replying.

If you don't have access to expensive media software like Cision, you can always pull together lists yourself through things you're already doing such as visiting the media site, reading their publication, or watching the shows themselves. If you spot someone who you think might work, check them out on Twitter and see what they're talking about. I can't emphasize this enough: make sure you are pitching the right person for your topic.

Book Media and Other Focused Media: Following the Beat

I have authors who only want to pitch book media, and that's fine most of the time, but consider whether your book media target does more than just feature books for review. If they don't, you may want to move on to another media target, because if you aren't pitching them your book within their review window, it won't get considered anyway.

And what about other focused media? Yes! If there is an editor or producer who has a focused beat on, let's say, medical, or political, or whatever else might be relevant to your pitch, go after them with your story.

Is Pitching Multiple People at One Outlet Okay?

I know that people do this, even PR folks (who should know better), but I generally don't recommend it. If you do find yourself going after several folks at the same publication, I recommend giving them the heads-up that you've also pitched so-and-so at their magazine or show or whatever. Why? Because you don't want them to be blindsided when they go into a story meeting with your email and find out several other folks got the same story, too.

Follow Up, Follow Up

When is it okay to be a pest and follow up on your pitch? Well, while it's never okay to be a pest, it is okay to do some follow-up. I generally recommend formulating another pitch for their considerationg, rather than sending an email saying "Did you get xxx?" It's how I always follow up—unless they've requested materials, or more information, in which case a regular follow-up email is fine.

If you've pitched media outlets and hear nothing, it doesn't mean they didn't get your email, it means that they got it and there was no interest. Media outlets won't give you feedback on what they liked or didn't like about your piece. They simply won't respond. Keep in mind that just because they didn't respond to your pitch that you can't pitch them again and again. If they don't want to hear from you, or if they have changed beats and are no longer covering that area, they will probably let you know.

Press Kits and Press Releases

There's a time and place for everything, but the time for press kits is really long gone. The last time I used an actual paper kit was maybe six or seven years ago. You can always put it online but having a press kit to mail is just a bit old school and, frankly, a waste of paper. The media will discard them almost every time, as it is too much clutter. Don't waste your time and money. You can put the kit on your website, and direct media there with a simple link.

What about press releases? In a world with nonstop breaking news, I say choose your release topics carefully. Press releases are fine as long as you have real news to share. The problem is that many times I see press releases being used to announce the release of a new book or product. If you have a big customer base, a huge mailing list, or a lot of fans hungry for your new stuff, it may make sense. Otherwise save your time and your news contacts and connections for when you have something really big to announce. It's very rare that the media picks up news from a release, or maybe on slow news days you might get a hit or two, but again, I probably wouldn't waste my time or theirs.

Your Media Room

Now here's something that can really help spice up your website. An online media room is a great place to store things like your bio, headshot, and links to any media you've been interviewed for or featured on. Online media rooms don't have to be complicated or involved, but they can be an interesting and informative page on your website, and a nice one-stop-shop where you can put all of your media materials, plus everything an interviewer might need for your upcoming gig. One final idea for your media room is to include a list of topics you can speak about, in case a media person finds you and wants to see what she or he might want to discuss with you!

While getting media coverage is harder these days, the rewards of ongoing media attention can be tremendous, and once you get into the rhythm of what to pitch, how, and when to pitch it, it could become some of the most enjoyable work you will do. Before you know it, ideas will start popping, and you may soon find that the sky's the limit in terms of opportunities in getting the word out!

Finding the Perfect Keywords
For Your Book!

*"I am a great believer in luck, and I find that the harder
I work, the more I have."*
– Thomas Jefferson

If people were looking online for your book, what keywords, or search terms, would you want them to use? Or rather, what keyword or words would you expect to be found under?

Confused? Here's a tip: first, figure out the top five to ten books in your market, and then go to Google and plug in the keywords you think would be associated with your book and see whether those top five to ten books come up. You should also search competition's websites to see what they rank for. Ideally, these are the keywords that you want to be associated with.

These keywords can (and probably some of them should) be used in your book title, subtitle, book description, and metadata, among other things.

1. _____

2. _____

3. _____

4. _____

5. _____

6. _____

7. _____

8. _____

9. _____

10. _____

The Amazon Factor

Every author I know wants a high rank on Amazon, but what's the best way to achieve it? When I first wrote *How to Sell Your Books by the Truckload* on Amazon.com, I looked at the various algorithms that helped a book rank better on that site. One of them was keywords. One of most important bits of research when plotting your keywords should be to see what's ranking well on Amazon in your subject matter or niche.

Here's a quick way to find out what's hot on this mammoth book site. First off, head over to the Amazon search bar and select 'books' in the drop down category. You want to search only for Kindle e-books on Amazon, since e-books are not restricted to the same categories and keywords as the traditional publishing world.

Then, start to type in your topic. We'll use finance as an example. Type in the word "finance," and you'll start to see a bunch of suggestions pop up.

Now let's take this a step further and type in your topic name ("finance" in this case) followed by one letter of the alphabet. For example, when I typed in "finance a," I pulled up: finance and investing, finance accounting, and finance advice, to name a few. You can keep going down the alphabet, typing in "finance b," "finance c," and so forth.

What will you do with these keywords once you have them? Well, just like I mentioned above, you'll want to use them in your book description, subtitle, even your title if you can.

You'll start to see these keyword search strings, which is a combination of characters and words, come together. You'll be able to look at each one to determine which are the best fits for your book in terms of content—as well as in terms of competition. Aim to use keywords similar to the ones used by books from your competitors with strong rankings. In a world where 4,500 books are published every day, even if their numbers sound high, a Kindle store rank 50,000-100,000 is strong.

Finding popular search terms for books on Amazon is a must these days. Though Google will help you get a good general idea of what folks are searching for, Amazon zeros in on what people are searching for as it relates to book buying, which is ultimately what you should care about.

Determining Your Book Category

"A great book should leave you with many experiences and slightly exhausted at the end. You live several lives while reading it."
– William Styron

Where will your book be found in a bookstore, library, or online? What category or categories will readers look at while searching for a book on your subject? While most reading this book will say "business" or "self-help," there might be sub-niches or other more specific subjects or categories where your book is more likely to be discovered. Keep in mind that the broader your category is, the more competition you'll have. The more narrow and niche-oriented your category, the more specific your audience, and the easier your book will be to find and sell.

Sometimes it's tough to determine the right category, so I've broken the process down in the following exercise:

In this first section, write down all the most relevant categories you can think of for your book. Once you've done that, we'll put them in order of importance!

Now, take the list you have created and head over to a bookstore (or do a search online) to be sure you're on the right track. In fact, a lot of authors love doing this exercise in a bookstore so they can search data right on the spot. Rank your categories by most relevant to least relevant. This will help you to determine where your book should go in a bookstore, and if you're still not sure after you're done, go ask an industry professional, or better yet, a bookstore manager!

1. _____

2. _____

3. _____

4. _____

5. _____

Putting Your Book to Work

Now that you've completed your book and learned some important marketing concepts to help sell it, consider the wondrous things it can do for you.

For example, you want to always have something that leads readers to look for more information. One idea is to capture newsletter or leads information by offering a sign-up bonus (such as bonus e-books, free guides, a workbook, or a class discount), or a way to go deeper into the content. You'll notice that in the book you're reading, I've included ways for you to dive into different layers of the content. It also helps to not overload the book with too much detail. I provided links back to my website in order to lead readers to a backend where they can access all sorts of content and in-depth instruction to help hem get published. You can do the same thing.

Also, if your goal is to get more speaking engagements, include speaker selling points such as topics, as well as ways to contact you, in the back of your book. But whether or not you want to bring readers in for more information, or for them to book you for a speaking engagement, you must have your contact points in the book.

Remember: make it easy for people to contact you. Don't make them think or dig or have to search for ways to reach you!

Great Book Descriptions Can Help Authors Sell More Books

Whhether they appear on Amazon or any other e-tailer, book descriptions are more important than most authors realize. They don't just show up on the back of your book, they show up everywhere! Many times I'll see blocks of text pulled from the back of the book and while in theory its not a bad idea, it may not be the greatest if your book description isn't strong to begin with. Maybe the book details are just slapped up on Amazon (or Barnes & Noble, and others) without an eye toward things like spacing, bulleting, and bolding.

In this section, I'm going to share some ideas about book descriptions specifically, and then some tips you may want to consider in order to enhance your own book description for the maximum punch on Amazon. Keep in mind, though, that most, if not all, of these tips can be used on any e-tailer.

Is Your Message Getting Through?
Spoiler alert: very few readers read word for word!

Most people don't read websites, they scan. Therefore, the same can be expected for your book description. If you have huge blocks of text without any consideration for spacing, bolding, bullets, or some other form of highlighting that helps the reader scan, many readers will just give up and move on, and you will have lost a sale.

Things like short paragraphs, highlighting, bolding, bullets, and special spacing are also much more visually appealing, and psychologically they invite the reader to delve in instead of to click off.

Book design (meaning the actual font on the pages) adopts this strategy, too. By having wide margins and spacing, bullets, and even boxed-in pieces to highlight particular text, the design invites the reader to read instead of taking inventory via a quick scan before moving on.

Our minds are image processors, not text processors, so huge, page-long chunks of text overwhelm the mind and, in fact, slow down the processing of your message considerably. On websites, people's attention span is even shorter than it is while reading a book. Even on sites like Amazon, where consumers go to buy, and often spend a lot of time comparing products and reading reviews, it's important to keep in mind that most potential readers will move on if your text is too cumbersome.

Then how can you make your description more scan-friendly?

- **Headlines:** the first sentence in the description should be a grabber, something to really pull the reader in. This text could also be a stunning blurb, or some kind of endorsement, but regardless, it should be in bold face. If you're looking at your Amazon book page, you could also use the "Amazon Orange" to set it apart from the rest of the text.

- **Paragraphs:** Keep paragraphs short at 2-3 sentences max.

- **Bolding:** You can bold face text throughout the description. In fact, I recommend it. Just be sure you aren't bolding too much, be strategic with them. For example, don't bold face 2-3 sentences in a row, because it'll have more impact if you just do a few key words or one sentence at most.

- **Bullets:** If your book is nonfiction, it's not a bad idea to bullet your information as much as possible. Take key points and the "here's what you'll learn" elements, and put them into a bullet point section that's easy to scan and is also visually appealing.

Use Code to Enhance Your Amazon Book Description and Headline

Want to know how to update the text styles within your book description? There are several types of code you can use to enhance your headline and description. Keep in mind that you can't make these changes to your headline using Author Central; it all has to be done from your Amazon author dashboard. Though making these changes won't affect your algorithm, per se, it will help make your book description more visually appealing.

Here are some of the coding enhancers available:

- **Bold**: The text you want bolded
- *Italics*: <i>The text you want italicized</i>
- Headline: <h1>The text you want for a headline</h1>
- Amazon Orange Headline: <h2>The text you want bolded</h2>

You can add in numbered lists and bullet points in order to enhance your book description.

Answering Readers' Biggest Question: "What's In It For Me?" – Fiction vs. Nonfiction

The biggest challenge authors face is writing a book description that highlights its benefits for readers, and does it in a way that's easy to understand, and inviting. This matters whether it's fiction or nonfiction, and it's a critical part of any book description. Remember, since there are 4,500 books published every day in this country, you can't afford to have a vague, dry, or boring book description. You must state clearly why this book is the best one they can buy.

Which leads me to the differences between fiction and nonfiction book descriptions.

- **Nonfiction**: First off, it's probably very likely that whomever you are targeting already owns ten or more titles similar to the one you just wrote. So why on earth should they add yours to their collection? While you're powering through your book description, keep in mind that you're likely serving a very cluttered market, and you'll need to be extremely and specifically clear about why your book matters. You should hook the reader from the first sentence, and remember to make a personal connection with the reader via the book description. You can do this by relating directly to your reader with verbiage such as: "Have you ever….?" Or using humor to pull them in, which I've seen done a lot with parenting books. Often, asking a question will get you to where you need to be, but ask a question you already know the answer to. For example, I have a book called *5 Minute Book Marketing for Authors* and the lead sentence asks: "Do you feel like you have zero time to market your book?"

What if you have a massively strong bio that helps carry the topic of the book in some substantial way? Let's say you're the head of research at a major institution regarding XYZ topic. That information should be factored into your book description. Keep it brief so that you'll have the chance to elaborate on it later.

Developing Your Elevator Pitch

Okay, what is an elevator pitch, and why do you need one? An elevator pitch is a one- to-two-sentence description of your book. It's the briefest of the briefest descriptions you can develop. Elevator pitches are important because people have an ever-shrinking attention span, and you need to capture someone's attention with a very short, succinct pitch.

Why does this matter for your book description? Starting with a short blurb or pitch is an excellent way to begin building your book description. Also, elevator pitches focus on the core of your book—the one element that your book could not omit—and that will be the biggest piece that matters to your reader.

Keep Your Verbiage Simple and Straightforward

When it comes to writing a book description, I encourage you to save your five-dollar words for another time. Effective book descriptions tend to use simple language that any layperson can understand. If you make someone think about a word, you'll lose them, and the rest your book description will go unread.

How Excited Are You? And How Excited Will Your Readers Be?

Have you ever seen a book description with a ton of exclamation points or caps? Much like in email, it feels like the person is screaming at you. Though I don't recommend eliminating exclamation points entirely for a book description, they should be used sparingly. I'd recommend one or two at most. Studies have shown that an exclamation point used here and there can help make a sentence seem even more authentic. In terms of all caps, don't even bother. Using all caps in a book description, or capitalizing what you consider important words, makes you look like an amateur. Overuse of quotation marks, especially for "scare quotes," does the same thing.

Spell Check

It goes without saying, but still I've seen it left undone often enough to feel like I need to say it. Please don't put up a book description full of typos; even one is too many.

Is Your Book Part of a Series?

If your book is a series, be sure to tell readers it is, and add that right to the headline. I also recommend that you make it part of the title, too. For example you might word your book title like this: *Deadly Heat: Heat Series, Book 4 of 7.*

Here's an example of Dan Silva's book—in terms of putting it in the actual book title:

The Black Widow (Gabriel Allon Series Book 16)
Kindle Edition
by Daniel Silva ▼ (Author)

Readers (especially fiction readers) love a series, so tell them right up front that your book is part of the same or similar story.

Include Top Keywords

Keywords are as important to your Amazon book page as almost anything else. I've written a lot about Amazon-specific keywords that you can read here (*Demystifying Amazon Categories, Themes, and Keywords* – Part 1 and Part 2, and *How to Sell Books by the Truckload on Amazon.com*), but here is a quick overview:

The term "keyword" is actually inaccurate, because readers don't search based on a single keyword. Think instead of keyword strings or phrases. So, for example, romance about second chances has been a popular search string on Amazon for a while now. However, by taking that sentence and inserting it into your book description, you can really help boost your visibility on the site, as well as keying into your readers' direct interest. So if they're searching for romance second chances, and they see it in the book description, it's going to ping them with: "Oh! This is the exact book I've been looking for."

That said, it's a good idea to avoid overstuffing your book description with keywords. I recommend settling on six or seven strings and using them sparingly throughout.

Don't Market to Your Ego

I often tell authors that no one cares that they wrote a book. Even family and friends may care, but they aren't your intended audience. If you want to pull in readers—and a lot of them at that—make sure your book appeals to **their** needs and **their** interests, not **yours**. This is partially why I never recommend that authors write their own book descriptions. I often hire someone to do it for me, because I'm just too close to it to see what **really matters** to my reader.

Tailor Your Bio to Your Book

One of things I see a lot is author bio information that has nothing to do with the book. For example, let's say you wrote a book about marriage, but your bio talks about how you live in Maine with your wife and three dogs. That doesn't really help substantiate your expertise for writing this book. The same is true for fiction, actually.

If you have multiple books, mention them. If you have a fun or quirky writing habit, mention that, too. It's a good idea to personalize this for your audience and your target market, to make sure what they're interested in, or what they'd ask before they hire you to do—say, repair work for them (if you're writing a DIY repair book, for example)—and talk about that. List any credentials as they may relate to the book topic and/or any research you've done. Most of all, make it interesting, and keep it short. Long, boring author bios don't sell books.

Include Quotes and Reviews

So often I see quotes such as: "This is the best mystery book I've read in ages!" but who actually said it is left out. Reviews and quotes/ endorsements/blurbs are fantastic to use in your book description, but only if they are cited appropriately. Several authors told me that they often don't cite them because they feel the name won't lend the kind of credibility they want from the favorable comment (for example, a quote from someone at work, or a neighbor). In that case, it would be more helpful for them to review the book instead.

Update Your Page Often

Here's something you may not have considered—your page doesn't have to be static. In fact ideally, it shouldn't be. When you get great quotes from experts' endorsements, reviews, and awards, update your book page to include them. And here's an idea...if you're doing a special promotion, book promo, discount or whatever, why not mention it in your product page book description (see screenshot below) on Amazon, and other platforms like Barnes & Noble?

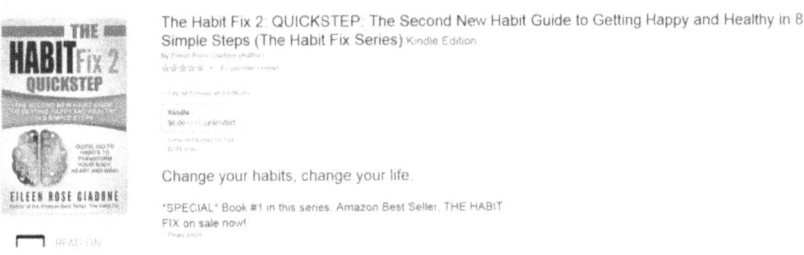

And last but not least, take a look at the following book description from Dan Silva. It's a great example that combines great review quotes with a book description that pulls you in from the first sentence. Book review quotes and endorsements are eye candy, i.e. people like what other people like. Even if you don't have quotes from reviews appearing in highly recognizable publications such as *Booklist* and *Publishers Weekly*, you should still add the ones you do have (just be sure to include the name of the reviewer and publication).

Notice how Silva's quotes in the description below are in bold face to draw attention to them? And check out the second paragraph.

Whoever wrote this book description inserted a quote from a review to help bolster the character description, which is another terrific idea.

"Fascinating, suspenseful, and bated-breath exciting.... Silva proves once again that he can rework familiar genre material and bring it to new life."
— *Publishers Weekly*, starred review

"Silva builds suspense like a symphony conductor.... A winner on all fronts."
— *Booklist*, starred review

Bestselling author Daniel Silva delivers another spellbinding international thriller—one that finds the legendary Gabriel Allon grappling with an ISIS mastermind.

Gabriel Allon, the art restorer, spy, and assassin described as the most compelling fictional creation "since Ian Fleming put down his martini and invented James Bond" (*Rocky Mountain News*), is poised to become the chief of Israel's secret intelligence service. But on the eve of his promotion, events conspire to lure him into the field for one final operation. ISIS has detonated a massive bomb in the Marais district of Paris, and a desperate French government wants Gabriel to eliminate the man responsible before he can strike again.

Book descriptions, whether on Amazon, iTunes, or Barnes & Noble, are your sales pitch. Ultimately, they are what will, or won't, help sell your book. Make sure they're tightly written, exceptionally engaging, and, most of all, able to turn a browse into a buy.

Winning the Name Game

"If you can't annoy somebody, there is little point in writing."
– Kingsley Amis

Choosing your book's title can be tricky; ask anyone who has spent any time at all trying to play the name game. It can be perplexing … and it will often determine the future of your book.

As I mentioned previously, keywords aren't just for the Web. Including keywords in your title makes it easy for anyone to decide that you are indeed covering a particular subject, and starting your title with a keyword can be the best of all. A good title should draw attention away from all the other books sitting on the shelf around it. It should be enticing, thought–provoking, and anything but dull. It should also be highly benefit-driven. Potential readers should know right from the start what the book is about, and why it will benefit them to have that information.

In other words, you need to target your audience with your title. Ask yourself who's going to be buying your book and what their age group is. When in doubt, visit a bookstore and scan some other titles in your niche, or take an afternoon and bury yourself in magazine covers. You can often compile a list of great titles from magazine covers; in fact, you'll get a great lesson in naming your book. If you look at the cover of a magazine, you'll see how savvy copy editors have managed to encompass all the elements (i.e. reading benefits) of that particular issue in just a few short phrases or sentences.

If you're still stumped for a book title, try naming three of the biggest problems your book helps readers solve. You've just come up with three more possible titles or chapter headings. Write them down and let them simmer in the back of your mind for a while, then experiment until you come up with an unusual play on words.

Brainstorm ideas with your friends. Give them three possible titles and ask them to choose their favorites. Scan titles and chapter headings in other books. Borrow a word here, a clever turn of phrase there. Keep massaging the title until you come up with something you like and, most importantly, something that others like.

Some of the most successful titles answer the typical reader's question of "What's in it for me?" or "Why should I care?" People want books that will inspire, educate, calm, enlighten, humor or entertain. Choose a title that answers those two questions, and you're well on your way.

If you're writing an advice book, the title can explain outcomes and even a timetable for achieving them—for example, *25 Things You Can Do This Week To Save Thousands Next Year*.

Here are a few original titles, followed by the titles that actually made it:

Tomorrow is Another Day ... *Gone With the Wind*
Blossom & the Flower ... *Peyton Place*
Something that Happened ... *Of Mice and Men*
John Thomas & Lady Jane ... *Lady Chatterley's Lover*

Something to Consider ...

Did you know that, whether for themselves or someone else, women buy the majority of books on the market? Designing a cover that grabs the attention of a woman is probably not a bad idea.

Did You Know?

Bookstore databases typically only store the first 30 characters of a book title. So if you have a name that's longer than 30 characters, guess what? It gets cut off. That's why a lot of publishers will reverse the name of a book, especially if it's nonfiction, so the subject matter comes first. For example, *Get Published Today!* was originally *An Author's Guide to On-Demand Publishing*. Had I kept the original title, it would have left a lot of people wondering, "*An Author's Guide* … to what?"

How to Price Your Book
for Optimal Success

*"Many of life's failures are people who did not realize
how close they were to success when they gave up."*
– Thomas Edison

Sometimes the simplest thing you can do to give your book a boost is to play around with the price.

It's one thing to have written a book, and it's quite another to have written one that actually sells. You have probably heard this from other indie authors, or even experienced it yourself. Your book gets added to Amazon, full of pomp and circumstance, and then: nothing. It's disheartening to see your hard work just sit there. But here's the good news: it might be an easy fix.

How you price your book is something we don't often think of as a trigger for book promotion or how to sell more books, but it should be. First, let's look at two important factors: your book's perceived value versus the going market rate.

Look at Other books

First and foremost, see what others are charging in your market. You may be surprised what you find out. It's never a good idea to price your book outside of what the market can bear, even if you toiled over the book, worked endlessly, lost sleep, and otherwise turned your life inside-out to get it written.

My Book Is Worth More!

Yes, I know. Your book is worth a heck of a lot more. In fact, if you add up all the hours you spent working on it, you probably couldn't charge enough for it. Here's the thing, though: you can't focus on your worth or your book's worth. You have to focus on what the market will bear.

Consider the E-book

In general, I find that most traditional publishers don't know how to price an e-book. I'll see e-books priced at $9.99, and up which is a powerful deterrent for most readers, partly because reader perception is that e-books have much lower production costs, and the price should reflect that. As you build your author marketing plan, keep in mind that e-books should not be priced as high as their print counterparts. Even pricing them within a dollar or two of a $14.95 book is too high.

I have talked to the folks at KDP (Kindle Direct Publishing) about this. They've told me their "sweet spot" for pricing e-books (in terms of what they see gets the most traction on their site) is between $2.99 and $5.99. Now, while these numbers might horrify you, keep in mind that deciding to price your book to suit your market will actually help encourage a potential reader to buy your book, rather than discourage them, and likely send them off to find a book more within their price range.

Price rotation

Now here's where the pricing strategy really gets interesting. When was the last time you changed the price of your book on Amazon? And I'm not talking about a price drop for an e-book promo, I'm talking about playing with your pricing. So, for example, I cited the price range of $2.99 to $5.99, and while you may disagree with it, why not give it a shot for a week or so?

Changing your book price can help spike your exposure on Amazon, because it triggers the Amazon internal algorithms. Sometimes I work with authors who will shift their book pricing regularly, from $5.99 down to $2.99 down to $1.99 and then back up again. I would, however, be careful about doing this too often. You don't want to be shuffling your book price two or three times in a week. Take a page from stores and how they run their sales. If you go into a department store, there is always something on sale, but never the same item priced differently three different times in a week. Ideally, I'd recommend experiment with how you price your book once a month, or more often if you're running an e-book promo that you're advertising.

Free E-books

I love free e-books—and while a lot of people feel like giving away books doesn't help book sales, I disagree. I've seen it help book sales a lot...as long as they are used strategically. I would also recommend that you consider having at least one consistently free (called permafree), or, if you have several titles, keep them in a promotion rotation. This works especially well when you have four or five books. If you decide to do a free promotion, know that despite the Amazon muscle behind a free e-book, you still have to promote it on your own, too. Try using hashtags, and also promoting it to sites like BookGorilla and Ignite Your Book. Doing even smallish paid advertisements can help out enormously.

Price promos

Whenever you do a downward price rotation, be sure to let your potential readers know you're running a sale. If you have a Super Fan group, whether it's a Facebook group or an email list, be sure to give them a heads-up too. Whenever I reduce a price on a print or e-book, I always, always do a promo, even if it's just a small one, to let folks know I'm running a sale.

Permafree E-books

I adore permafree for the simple reason that if you have three or more books, having a free one can really boost the sales of your other titles—in some cases increasing sales by three or four times what they were selling before. So what is "permafree?" It's an e-book that's always free on Amazon. And while you can't put a free e-book onto the site itself, you can ask Amazon to price match it. Generally what I'll do is recommend an author pick either their oldest book (as long as it's still relevant and current) or the first book in a fiction or nonfiction series, and make that book free. In order to do this, you have to publish it everywhere, which is easy to do with sites like Draft2Digital and Smashwords. Just upload your book there and make it free. Those sites will publish the book on Nook, iTunes, Kobo, and everywhere else you tell them to publish it.

Once the book is free on these sites, let Amazon know by clicking the "tell us about a better price" link just under the book details on your Amazon page (note: sometimes it takes a few tries to get Amazon to recognize it's free elsewhere). Once the book is free, you'll begin to see it surging up the Amazon ranks (under free e-books). Just make sure there's a simple page in the back of your free book that invites readers to check out your other titles, and include links to these titles so they can easily find (and buy) them.

As you will discover over the course of marketing your book, so many factors come into play with author publicity and book promotion campaigns. Ultimately, though, adjusting your book's price can make a huge difference in your book's overall sales, and what you earn from those sales. If you need a boost, or while you reexamine the things you're doing to sell your book, consider periodically revisiting how you price your book. Bookmark this page so you can easily reference the information while as you continue executing your book marketing plan.

Your Marketing and Publication Timeline

*"Strategy and timing are the Himalayas of marketing.
Everything else is the Catskills."*
– Al Ries

They say that timing is everything, and it's especially true for book promotion. Once your book is available, the clock starts ticking. You've decided how you are publishing your book and setting it up for success, you'll need to decide when, where, and how you're going to implement your marketing plan. Here's a brief outline of what you should plan to do and when:

While the Book Is Being Printed

- ✓ Begin to pull together a media list
- ✓ Determine your hook or hooks
- ✓ Start highlighting promotional dates on a calendar
- ✓ Put together your digital press kit
- ✓ Make sure your website and/or book page is up and running and ready to go for your book launch
- ✓ Put together your association list for any potential public speaking opportunities
- ✓ Decide when to notify your customers, whether you'll do a full launch or a soft launch, giving them an exclusive chance to buy a copy of your book early

Four Months Prior to Publication Date

✓ Send packets out with promotional materials for signings or speaking events to coincide with your release date. These can be emailed or mailed, depending on how the receiver wants to view them

✓ Prepare and send packets with your book to prepublication date reviewers

✓ If you're going after the national magazine or national TV show markets, send out emails with links to the detailed information on your web site.

Three Months Prior to Publication Date

✓ If you have a topic worthy of major media attention, pitch it now, so your interview will coincide with the release date of your book (especially with magazines and television, talk shows in particular, it's best to approach them 3-6 months before your launch date).

✓ Start a list of potential media contacts and activities for local promotion

One Month Prior to Publication Date

✓ Make sure media contacts are current—add to them if necessary

✓ Start pitching yourself to radio

✓ Start pitching yourself to the newspaper market

✓ Confirm signings and other events

Your Book Is Available

✓ Start pitching radio shows for interviews

✓ Plan media announcements around signings and events

✓ Submit book to post-publication-date reviewers

✓ If you haven't already done so, notify your customers that you have a book

Ongoing Promotional Activities

✓ Keep pitching radio

✓ Pitch holidays and special events appropriate to your topic

✓ Keep pitching yourself to speaking events and signings

✓ Send thank-you notes as appropriate for ongoing activities

✓ Keep doing whatever you can, as long as it makes sense for your book!

Audience Questions Spark Great Ideas

Watching someone speak can help spark your own ideas. I get a lot of my blog, book, or article ideas from the Q&A segment of my own talks, but also when listening to others do the same. Try attending a session on a similar topic, and if you can't find something that's in your area, see if you can find a few clips of a talk on YouTube or TED Talks. Audience questions can give you some great ideas for your book and media pitches.

Getting Your Book into Bookstores

"A bookstore is one of the only pieces of evidence we have that people are still thinking."
– Jerry Seinfeld

If I gather ten authors in a room and ask them their highest goals for their books, the first is usually getting onto a best-seller list, and the second is getting into bookstores. The tricky part about bookstores, though, is that the number of titles released every year continues to grow, but bookstore shelf space and bookstores in general keep shrinking.

7% of books published generate 87% of total retail sales
1187 of titles sell 50,000 or more copies
93% of all books published sell less than 1,000 copies

The Realities of Shelf Space

First, let's look at the realities of getting on the shelf. Keep in mind that the numbers I'm about to cite are not meant to discourage you, but rather to give you some insight into the competition that exists within bookstore walls.

When it opens, the average Barnes & Noble carries approximately 100,000 new titles. The average number of new titles that a Barnes &

Noble buys a year is 25,000. This number might seem high to you, but when you factor in that the big six generate (on average) 24,150 new titles a year, this number seems quite small. Also, backlist is a big seller in bookstores. So much so, that 75% of the inventory is backlist and represents 65% of sales.

What does this mean for you and your book? First and foremost, it means the ability to get into a store is limited by the fact that much of the shelf space in bookstores is bought and paid for by the New York publishers. By that, I mean that endcaps, table displays, and the average book on the shelf are all intentionally placed there. Very little in a bookstore is accidental. Additionally, bookstore numbers are shrinking by going out of business, so this shelf space and endcap space is even more crucial to big name publishers.

Okay, now you know the numbers, let's break down some creative ways to get into bookstores, or to learn from them. Because bookstores can teach us a lot!

S-P-E-L-L It Out

Readers don't want to be told. Don't say "Get a website" and then leave them to guess the how and why. Show them how. Don't just mention that they need to do XYZ, tell them how. Give tips, how-tos, and, if possible, detailed walk-throughs. If you can't do that, or if you feel it'll take up too much space in the book with tedious detail, then send them to where they can get it (notice how we've directed readers to restricted-access pages on our website). Spelling it out will make your book much easier to understand and use. Your book should hold the reader's hand, and give them a guide to follow. If you truly help your readers, you'll have a great book.

Marketing Secrets of a Bookstore (aka How to Get Bookstore Placement For Your Book)

"I went to a bookstore and asked the saleswoman,
'Where'sthe self-help section?' She said if she told me,
it would defeat the purpose."
– George Carlin

As I mentioned in the previous chapter, although top author goals for their books include appearing on a best-seller list and getting book placement in a traditional brick and mortar bookstore, there are challenges associated with both, given the sheer number of books published each year, both independently and by the Big Six.

Although many independent stores continue to flourish, bookstores want books that are already selling, especially regionally. With that said, a visit to your local bookstore can accomplish more than just pitching your book for stocking consideration. They also offer a wide range of opportunities for learning, and for building your book marketing plan.

So turn a visit to your local bookstore into a research project. It's one of the best lessons you'll ever get in book marketing. Here's how to break it down:

Know Your Market

First, if you've written a book for which there is no market (read: there are no books out there catering to your audience), you have a problem. Unless you are already a brand, meaning you're a published author with a significant following, it's unlikely that you will be able to create enough momentum for a yet-unserved market that a publisher would consider you. If it hasn't been written, there is likely a reason why.

Now there are always exceptions of course. *Red Hot Internet Publicity – Fourth Edition* (2016) is not a title I would have published in 1976, mostly because there was no Internet back then. So, yes, new markets are developing all the time, but it's key to wait till those markets emerge—otherwise you're selling to an audience that doesn't exist.

This also goes for creating a new genre or niche for your book. You should fit into an existing one, and find the best one for your target audience. This is also crucial, since sometimes books can straddle different markets. A change in title can take your book written for women wanting to succeed in business and move it from the business category into self-help and/or spirituality. Be clear about where your book belongs. Remember, a confused mind won't make a choice, so if you confuse your potential reader, you're likely to lose a sale.

Who Else Is Sharing Your Shelf Space?

Understanding what your market is, and who else as far as competition is sharing your shelf space is essential. What are their books like, and have you read them?

This is all part of your market research: know your competition, and know who shares your space. It is not just important to know about other competing titles. Knowing everything possible about your competition is key for marketing and media positioning as well.

Also, you should take note of all other recent titles in your category and go visit their websites. If you're really eager to keep an eye on your competition, you could also get an alert through TalkWalker or Mention triggered by their name or book title, so you can see how much traction they're getting. (For more information on these services, check out the When to Publish chapter.) I will usually do this for any major author in my market, as well as for all their book titles. Not only can you keep an eye on their hit rate, but these sites and media targets could be good marketing and selling opportunities for you as well.

Every Book Tells a Story

Every book in your subject area will tell you a little something about the author and publisher. In this case, I'm not talking about the contents of the book itself. I'm talking about things like the cover, book jacket, book size (both dimensions and page count), as well as endorsements/reviews and back cover copy. Learning from books that are already out there and successful is a great way to position yours for success.

Books that make it onto a shelf in a bookstore do so because they "look" the part. Yes, your book may be the best out there, but if it doesn't meet the needs of your niche, if it doesn't look the part, it simply won't be shelved with the others. In order to play in the publishing sandbox, you must play by the rules. While it's nice to be a maverick, and to hear stories about authors who "bent the rules" and claimed success, you'll find that following the rules and playing to the market are the keys to success. There are 4,500 books published every day, and currently five million e-books on Amazon. Yes, you want to stand out, but you also need to look the part.

Bookstore Checklist

If you decide that having your book in a bookstore is still at the top of your goal list, here's a checklist to get you started. You'll want to expand on this as you find more titles or more ideas to research. I suggest, for example, adding in URLs from the book jacket so you can research the author's website.

- What niche or genre does your book fall into?

- Is there a subgenre/sub-niche and, if so, what is it? (for example, my books fall into reference/writing, writing being the subgenre)

- List the top five titles and authors in that market (niche/subject matter, genre, subgenre)

- What are the key points each book has in common? Was it that the cookbooks you studied had nutritional analysis on every page?

Reality Check: Getting Your Book Carried Locally

We once had an author who wanted his books to be carried in his local market. As it happened, he was self-published, and his local market was a top thirty media market, making it even more challenging to break into.

After a few weeks and many, many calls, we were happy to report that his book was now carried in six stores, including one large and well-known independent store in his area. When I reported this to him, he was discouraged: "Only six??" he asked, and was even more discouraged to learn some of the stores would only carry two two copies of his book. We talked for a while about the realities of bookstore placement, number of books published, and so on, but candidly, none of it seemed to matter.

After listening to the author vent, I turned the tables on him and said, "How about this: we know the odds. We wish you were in every store in your area, but the reality is you're not. At least not yet. So instead of looking at what you don't have, let's look at how we can maximize what you do have."

I went on to recommend that he go to each bookstore, sign books, and meet the staff who worked there (read: the people who could push his book). I also recommended that he meet the store manager as well. Why? Because for most booksellers, books are just books, faceless, and not connected to an author they will ever meet. But when you, the author, go into a store and shake their hand, sign books, and take the time to get to know the bookstore staff, they might be inclined to recommend your book to the buying public, which is what happened in this case. The staff at the bookstores he visited got to know him and, because of that, helped him sell his book. Eventually the reorders came, and other stores began to pick up his title.

Sometimes good marketing is just a matter of the old adage: turning lemons into lemonade. The perception he could have walked away with was: no one wants my book. Instead, I helped him turn his challenge into an opportunity, and consequently, he got what he wished for. Did it happen overnight? No, it did not. But it *did* happen, and in an age of everyone-can-publish, that's really something.

Getting Into Bookstores

Now you've done so much hard work, you're probably eager to see your book right alongside the others, right? There are a few ways to accomplish that.

Book Distributors

Book distribution is often handled by companies whose entire focus is to distribute your book to a variety of places, including bookstores. Many distributors have sales teams to help sell your book into stores and outlets. It's not easy getting a distributor, and most of them won't pick up an author with no track record. If you think you're ready for distribution, you can take a look at our resource section, which has a listing of distributors as well as pitching guidelines.

Pitching Bookstores Directly

Most stores have small press managers who will handle book submissions from small publishers or first-time authors. Barnes &

Noble has an office dedicated to this in New York, and those folks are the ones you'll pitch for stocking consideration. However, it does vary from store to store, so my suggestion is for you to call and ask you local store the best way for you to pitch to them before just dropping a packet in the mail.

Local Store Stocking

Many times, I find that authors can easily get a few of their books into local stores, especially if they are doing local promotion. You'll want to walk into your bookstore and ask to speak with the manager. He or she will be able to tell you what their guidelines are for carrying your book in their store.

When it comes to bookstores, sometimes the seemingly tedious process is worth the effort. If your goal is to see your book on the shelf of a store, then expect the process to take a little bit of time. Bookstores are pitched to a lot, and your book is likely one of many they are considering. That said, getting a buy-in is fantastic, and whether the store is stocking five copies of your book or one hundred, it's really great win all the way around.

Short is The New Long

When it comes to books, almost anything goes these days. But one key factor is that it must be helpful. I have books that are more than three hundred pages long, and others with fewer than fifty pages. In some cases, you may want to publish a lot of content, so several books might work better for your market.

Do You Want Your Book to be a Best-Seller?

If you ask any new author, they'll eagerly nod yes. But are best-seller lists still relevant? The emotional high, and the credibility gained from having a best-selling book can be fantastic, and certainly the mainstream publishing industry still gives a nod to a best-seller, but for how long? In 2016, there were no breakout best-sellers, like we've seen in years past. It may be that this is a trend. It's certainly worth watching. With so much weight and power shifting from traditional publishing to the independent side of things, book sales just aren't calculated the way they once were.

So does being a "best-seller" really mean more sales? Not necessarily, and here's why:

Best-seller lists are changing all the time. The rules are revised constantly, and the way books are ranked shifts regularly. This is largely due to the sheer number of books flooding the market. With 4,500+ books published daily, these lists simply cannot adapt to these changes.

Independently published books have the potential to affect the best-seller lists, especially if they hit big numbers. It's important to really understand the word "best-seller," because, as we've seen with the recent Amazon crackdown on using terms like "best-seller" on your book cover, it can be a slippery slope (read more on this here: www.amarketingexpert.com/kdp-amazon-best-seller-news/).

First off, the term "hit a list" can mean hitting a best-seller list at any point of entry, including the bottom 100. In fact, many books that "hit a list" are never viewed by consumers; they land on the list, stay for a week or so, and then vanish. The numbers and metrics for this can be tricky, and are not always entirely accurate. If you've ever tried to hit a list and found yourself disgusted with the odds, I hope this chapter sheds some light on the realities of how the process works.

How Best-Seller Lists Work

Best-seller lists vary by season, market, and genre or niche. Surprisingly enough, how many copies you need to sell to be a "best-seller" often depends on when you release it. Pre-Christmas releases, for example, require bigger numbers than May releases. Why? The hotter the month (not in temperature but in publishing releases), the harder it is to get onto a list.

Reporting is another key factor, especially because not all reporting is accurate and it could be slow to update. You could hit 20,000 sales in October, and not see the numbers until November. Moreover, sales reporting can also be inaccurate. Did you know that there's a whole market share that's never reported? Technical, scholarly, and law-related books can make up a large chunk of the book market, yet are never reported. Christian titles work the same way. You might say, "Well, what about *The Shack*?" This particular Christian title is different, and hit a list because it was sold en masse in retail outlets and not sequestered to Christian retailers who don't get the benefit of reporting to the lists.

Then there's the Amazon factor, and big box retailers, which complicate the "best-seller" issue further. Nielsen's BookScan is the keeper of the numbers and, according to my research, BookScan does not report on self-publishing companies like Createspace or Amazon's new KDP print book platform www.amarketingexpert.com/amazon-kdp-print-books/). They also don't include Sam's Club, WalMart, and Costco. Furthermore, BookScan cannot access all of Amazon's numbers, only sales that are directly tied to an ISBN. If your e-book publishes without an ISBN (using Amazon's ASIN system instead), BookScan cannot and does not count it.

Some sources say BookScan only reports on on 75 to 85% of sales, but I'd bet that number reported is actually lower than that. If you consider the lists of technical, scholarly, and law-related books, the Christian market, the millions of self-published titles every year, and all the e-books using Amazon's ASIN system, I'd wager a guess that BookScan gets maybe 65-70% of the market.

You might argue that indie and e-book-only books don't matter in the best-seller counts, and you could be right. That said, I recently spoke with an e-book-only indie author with 52 titles who sells 20k books per month. While that 20k number is high, it's divided among all of her books. Still, it's a reasonable assumption that counting her sales total via BookScan could be a game-changer. Add in other successful indie authors, and it could make a huge difference.

The Best-Seller Structure and How Lists Are Calculated

Every list pulls book data differently, and the *New York Times*, for example, does not pull book data from BookScan. Instead, how they've always done it, they cull their list by using a super-secret list of stores reporting from across the country. Their lists are specific to what's hot and selling in their select group of stores, and not at all based on BookScan numbers—which may be good, since we now know what BookScan reports and what they don't.

USA Today and *The Wall Street Journal* do, however, base their best-seller lists on BookScan's sales numbers. One fly in the ointment is that e-books are separated from print, because this can skew the numbers greatly. If an author sells large numbers each of their e-book and print versions, they might not hit a list, since the digital and print copies weren't tabulated together. While it's great that e-books are even being acknowledged in best-seller lists, I'm certain separating out those numbers has significantly impacted reporting.

As I said earlier, seasons can make a difference, along with any advance buzz. Publishing is often about perception, and any advance buzz that a book gets will help it land on a list. Generally, a book that is just "born" into the publishing world with no buzz or advance reviews won't capture the attention of a big list. The author might perform well locally, but generally not nationally, unless, like the *Fifty Shades* phenomenon, an online viral buzz builds.

Sales surges should also be considered. It often happens during a very short interval, and doesn't always have to equate to huge numbers. Instead the velocity of the push is what matters in such cases. A publishing associate of mine once told me that a book she was working with only sold 4,000 copies before it landed on a major list. The smallness of the number is staggering when you think about it. Factor in that, even knowing this book hit a list during a slow period, which worked in its favor.

Gray Areas, and Genres or Niches Not Reported

As I mentioned previously, certain genres or niches (namely Christian, technical, scholarly, and the like) aren't reported. And while many of them don't sell in big numbers, and perhaps it makes sense not to tally them, the other sticky piece is bulk purchases.

What's a bulk purchase? Let's say a book club wants to buy your book for their membership, and they purchase 10 copies from Amazon. If these 10 books are purchased from the same IP address, it counts as one book. By the same token, if big, bulk purchases of your book are legitimately bought by an organization for gifting to their members, or as a fundraiser for example, this number is also not counted by the Wall Street Journal, and, potentially, other lists as well.

Rigging a List

Some years ago, we worked on a book that hit a best-seller list, and it was incredibly exciting. Until someone discovered the author had bought up copies on their own in order to tweak the numbers.

Yes, you can, in fact, rig a best-seller list. There are companies who will buy up your book for you. You pay them a fee, and then another fee for the cost of the books and—voilá, a best-seller! How much does this cost? Well, upwards of $30,000 to $50,000. Is it worth it? Well for me, I'd rather hit a list the old-fashioned way, by writing a book that's so good it sells like hotcakes, but not everyone agrees with me. I've spoken to authors who are doing it, and while I am not a fan of achieving being on a list in this fashion, it seems to work for them.

Some years ago, you could contact 20,000 of your closest friends, ask them to go onto Amazon and buy up copies of your book and voilá—instant best-seller! It no longer works quite the same way, since Amazon caught on to the whole bulk/grouping buying thing. There was a time when the companies who existed for the sole purpose of buying up your book could really help you hit a list.

Does it Matter, Really?

Over the years, we've worked with a lot of best-sellers, and while it's fun, glamorous, and awesome to be a part of, for most indie authors it isn't reality. I see the list rules changing, and I see more and more indie authors succeeding with big sales numbers and literally killing it on their own. Would a best-seller status help them to ratchet it all up a notch? Probably. The problem is, most indie authors can't get there because the system isn't working in their favor.

The other piece of this is the cost. While there is the occasional book that will pop out and become a success after its release, most books need major, national pushes well before the book is out. Books sold into bookstores are reaching the point where they're reserved only for the brand name authors like Stephen King, Dean Koontz, James Patterson and Nora Roberts, or big, breakout books which are getting a lot of buzz. When it comes to hitting a national best-seller list, bookstores can still help those numbers along. If you aren't nationally distributed, if you haven't gone after long-lead, pre-publication reviews, you may want to set your dreams of a *New York Times* best-seller aside and focus instead on more productive and focused book marketing efforts.

What about Amazon? Truthfully, you could hit the Amazon best-seller list at any time. Your book doesn't have to be brand, spanking new. Just keep in mind that, of all the retailers out there, Amazon sees the bulk of what's being published, so competition will be fierce.

This chapter is not meant to be a buzzkill, nor do I want to tank your hopes and dreams of becoming a best-selling author. So many times I meet or work with authors who have one, singular focus: hitting a list. While that's great, it's just not always a realistic goal. Instead, spend your time building sales channels and building knowledge and connections that will last for the duration of your career. Those are the ingredients for an (eventual) best-seller.

Smile, You're on Candid Camera!

Another fun thing that businesses can do is start a conversation around unique uses for their product. For this you might interview consumers, or have them submit videos. See if you can have readers submit a fun video of unique ways they've used your book, or where your book has traveled (Did they take it on vacation with them to Italy?). Offer prizes to help incentivize readers to submit content!

Resources

Vendors and People We Love to Work With

Self-Publishing Tools

Book Cover Designers:
TLC Graphics – www.tlcgraphics.com
MonkeyCMedia – www.monkeycmedia.com

Book Production Company:
Girl Friday Productions – www.girlfridayproductions.com

Branding:
Jeniffer Thompson – MonkeyCMedia – j@monkeycmedia.com

Bar Code Suppliers:
AccuGraphiX – www.bar-code.com
Bar Code Graphics – www.barcode-us.com
BookMasters – www.bookmasters.com
FineLine Technologies – www.FineLineTech.com
Filmasters.com – www.filmasters.com
General Graphics – www.ggbarcode.com

Blogging Software:
Blogger.com – www.blogger.com
WordPress.com – www.wordpress.com
Typepad.com – www.typepad.com

Distributors to Libraries:

Quality Books, Inc. – www.quality-books.com
Unique Books – www.unique-booksinc.com/
Independent Book Publishers Association –
www.ibpa-online.org/resources/distributor-wholesalers/

Editing Services:

Faith Freewoman – Demon for Details Manuscript Editing –
www.demonfordetails.com
Robin Quinn – quinnrobin@aol.com
Editorial Freelancers Association – www.the-efa.org/index.php

Fulfillment Services:

Book Clearing House (BCH) / Nancy Smoller – www.bookch.com
Book Masters / Cathy Purdy – www.bookmasters.com

Ghostwriters

Business Ghost/Michael Levin – www.businessghost.com
Kevin Anderson and Associates –
ka-writing.com/ghostwriting-services/
Ghost Writer, Inc. – rainbowriting.com/ghostwriting-services/
Professional Ghost – www.professionalghost.com/

Printers, Offset:

BookMasters – www.bookmasters.com
Sun Graphics Book – book.sun-graphics.com/
McNaughton & Gunn – www.bookprinters.com
R.R. Donnelley & Sons – www.rrdonnelley.com/wwwrrd/Home.asp
Sheridan Books –www.sheridanbooks.com
Thomson-Shore, Inc. – thomsonshore.com/
Gorham Printing – www.gorhamprinting.com

Printers, Digital:
DeHart's Media Services / Don DeHart don@deharts.com –
www.DeHarts.com
Gorham Printing / Kathleen Shaputis
kathleens@gorhamprinting.com – www.gorhamprinting.com

Printers, Self-Publishing:
Lightning Source/Ingram Book Group –
www.ingramcontent.com/publishers/lp/lightning-source

Publishers, Self-Publishing:
Wheatmark – www.wheatmark.com
CreateSpace – www.createspace.com

Professional Organizations:
Independent Book Publishers Association – www.ibpa-online.org/
American Book Producers Association – www.abpaonline.org
American Booksellers Association (ABA) – www.bookweb.org
The Association of American Publishers (AA) –
www.publishers.org
The Authors Guild – www.authorsguild.org
Book Industry Study Group – www.bisg.org

Website Design:
Sublime Creations – www.sublimecreations.com/

Wholesalers:
Baker & Taylor – www.btol.com
Bookazine – www.bookazine.com
Ingram – www.ingram.com

Helpful Websites

Writing & Publishing Organizations

- Independent Book Publishers Association: A terrific organization to belong to, whether you've published one book or 20. It also has a yearly "Publisher's University," which precedes the Book Expo America. A not-to-be-missed educational and networking program! Visit www.ibpa-online.org/
- National Writers Union: The only union representing writers in all genres/niches, formats, and media working in the US market. Visit www.nwu.org.
- The Authors Guild: Offers several benefits, including e-mail alerts and bulletins, seminars, and a contract service department. The guild can also help you with rights, e-rights, copyright issues, and taxes. Membership requires that you've published at least one book or three articles. Visit www.authorsguild.org/.
- American Society of Journalists and Authors: Offers an annual conference, newsletter, writer referral service, professional resource lists, and online discussion forums. Visit asja.org/.

Publicity, Resources & Promotion

- Books XYZ: Looking for another outlet to sell and promote your book? Try Books XYZ. A basic listing is free. If you want to run your cover photo here, it's $25. You pay for your own shipping, but Books XYZ only requires a 15 percent commission on every sale. Visit www.booksxyz.com.
- Bookwire.com: This site helps keep you on top of what's going on in the industry. The site offers a section for promotion and event listings, plus regular e-mail updates. www.bookwire.com/

- Wordmuseum.com: A great resource to list your book, purchase advertising, or submit an author interview. wordmuseum.com/
- Writershelpdesk.com: A very useful website for authors, filled with links, reports and helpful advice. www.writershelpdesk.com/
- American Booksellers Association: A great site for locating bookstores and media materials. bookweb.org/
- Ignome Corporation: A great place to list your books for free. www.ignome.com/books/submission/
- Bookmarket.com: This site by John Kremer is a cornucopia of information to get you started and keep you going. bookmarket.com/
- Ideasiteforbusiness.com: Chock-full of great advice, although more general in nature. I always seem to come away with at least a kernel of new information. Sometimes that's all it takes. ideasiteforbusiness.com/
- Freelancewrite.about.com: A great resource for freelancers, with links and helpful tips about writing, publishing and marketing. Don't miss out on this one. freelancewrite.about.com/od/
- Authorsden.com: A great place for authors to show their stuff. Grab yourself a profile page and start telling the world about your book. While you're there, take a look at my page. www.authorsden.com/visit/author.asp?id=1221
- Schoolbookings.com: A great place to register if you're interested in obtaining speaking engagements at schools. schoolbookings.com/
- Tradepub.com: If you're looking for trade publications in your topic or area of expertise, you can browse its list of more than 300 publications. Subscriptions to its various trade publications are free to professionals who qualify. www.tradepub.com/

Media, Media, Media

- If you're looking for articles relevant to your topic or area of expertise, shoot on over to www.journalistexpress.com.
- Blue Eagle: Locating media professionals just got a bit easier. With links to more than 700 newspaper and magazine columnists, Blue Eagle at www.blueeagle.com is a terrific resource for any savvy PR pro.
- Mr. Magazine: Every month this magazine sleuth gives you the heads-up on which magazines are hot and which are not. Visit www.mrmagazine.com.
- If you're having a tough time locating an article that appeared in a daily newspaper because you don't know the name of the newspaper, then head on over to www.newspaperlinks.com, which has papers listed by state, city, and region. The site also links you to the newspapers' websites.
- No budget for a press-clipping service? Not to worry. Google has a great news site that will help you keep track of keywords, and when, where, and how you are mentioned in the news. Just go to www.news.google.com and click on "News Alerts." You'll need to supply the keywords to search for, and an e-mail address where they can the search results to. It's fast, easy and very thorough!

Publishing Info, Trends, and Updates

- Publishing Central: Helps you stay current on all the publishing news. Here you can learn about industry associations, current news, book trends, and book sales statistics. Visit www.publishingcentral.com.
- BookWire: Offers daily publishing news, literary events, and a wealth of industry links. Visit www.bookwire.com.
- Trend watching: A great newsletter that will help you stay on top of trends. The newsletter is free; just log onto the site at www.trendwatching.com to subscribe.

- Trend–spotting, anyone? If you're looking to stay one step ahead of the game, the following links will help you do just that. Each focuses on forecasting and future trends—great if you're looking to anchor your book on the latest hot, new thing. www.wfs.org – www.iftf.org – www.burrus.com – www.faithpopcorn.com

Research, Statistical, and Legalese-Related Sites

- Libraryspot.com: Great site for research! www.libraryspot.com/
- Findarticles.com: A vast archive of published articles you can search for free. I can't tell you how often I've used this site, and it's constantly updated. www.findarticles.com/
- Don't reinvent the wheel—instead, go to www.searchbug.com/legal/forms2.asp to find a terrific resource for legal forms, including subcontractor agreements, contracts and more!
- Yourdictionary.com: An excellent collection of dictionary portals. This site offers links to a huge selection of language dictionaries, including dictionaries for rare (vanishing) languages, a good selection of Native American language dictionaries, plus translation and grammar tools.
- Looking for some statistics straight from the government? Head on over to www.usa.gov/statistics
- Another dictionary that allows you to look up the meaning of a word from a variety of different sources is www.onelook.com. This dictionary will also help locate slang and medical dictionaries.
- Any research relative to the fifty states just got easier with www.50states.com/. It's a treasure trove of state-by-state information. Every time you click on one state, it will take you to a wealth of data helpful to any writer trying to get background info on a particular part of the country.

- Another great site for statistics about just about everything is www.statistics.com.
- Refdesk.com: Refers to itself as "the single best source for facts on the Net." There's an incredible list of dictionaries, almanacs, encyclopedias and much, much more.

Thank You for Reading!

Dear Reader,

I hope *The New Business Card* helped to set a new and exciting path for your professional future, and I hope you learned a lot!

The goal for this book is to share solid business advice to help others. So I hope you'll continue to pass these ideas forward, helping other business owners you may know who are also struggling with getting exposure, or want to build their speaking careers, or get more media.

It's all possible with a book!

Also, don't forget to download your free workbook here: www.amarketingexpert.com/the-new-business-card-workbook

Finally, I'd really appreciate a review.

Reviews are a huge help to authors and I'm not exempt from that. Loved it, hated it—I'd just like to hear your feedback because I can only provide the info I think you need, but I want to provide the info you feel you need as well. Your honest feedback will help everyone going forward!

Please also check out my author page, including my other books: amazon.com/author/therealbookgal

Wishing you much success!

Penny

Penny Sansevieri

Download Your Free Workbook

To get a free, downloadable file containing all of the worksheets and brainstorming elements of the book visit the below link:

www.amarketingexpert.com/the-new-business-card-workbook

Simply enter your email to have a copy sent to you instantly!

Schedule Your Discount Coaching Package

As a bonus I also want to give you a special discount on coaching while you develop your book!

Reserve 3 or more hours of coaching at once and receive $50 off per hour—that's a minimum of $150 in savings!

I'll help ensure you're making all the right decisions, and bringing a first-class product to market that reflects your unique offering.

But act fast if you're in a hurry, my calendar books quickly!

Simply email info@amarketingexpert.com and reference the "business card coaching package" to reserve your discount coaching.

About Penny C. Sansevieri &
Author Marketing Experts, Inc.

Penny C. Sansevieri, founder and CEO Author Marketing Experts, Inc. (AME), is a best-selling author and internationally recognized book marketing and media relations expert. She also is an adjunct professor of self-publishing at NYU.

Her company is a leader in the publishing industry and has developed some of the most innovative social media and Internet book-marketing campaigns. She is author of five books, including *Red Hot Internet Publicity*, which has been called "the leading guide to everything Internet."

AME is the first book marketing and publicity firm to use Internet promotion to its full impact through the Virtual Author Tour™. It strategically harnesses social networking sites such as Twitter, blogs, book videos, and other relevant resources, to push an author's message into the online community on sites related to the book's topic, and thereby position the author in his or her market.

AME has recently had eleven client books top bestseller lists, including *New York Times, USA Today,* and *Wall Street Journal*.

To learn more about Penny's books or her promotional services, visit her website at www.amarketingexpert.com.

www.ingramcontent.com/pod-product-compliance
Lightning Source LLC
Chambersburg PA
CBHW051310220526
45468CB00004B/1280